OPPOSING
VIEWPOINTS®
SERIES

Endangered Oceans

Other Books of Related Interest:

"Congress shall make
no law . . . abridging
the freedom of speech,
or of the press."

First Amendment to the U.S. Constitution

The basic foundation of our democracy is the First Amendment guarantee of freedom of expression. The Opposing Viewpoints Series is dedicated to the concept of this basic freedom and the idea that it is more important to practice it than to enshrine it.

OPPOSING VIEWPOINTS® SERIES

| Endangered Oceans

Louise I. Gerdes, Book Editor

WITHDRAWN

GREENHAVEN PRESS
A part of Gale, Cengage Learning

GALE
CENGAGE Learning™

Detroit • New York • San Francisco • New Haven, Conn • Waterville, Maine • London

Christine Nasso, *Publisher*
Elizabeth Des Chenes, *Managing Editor*

For more information, contact:
Greenhaven Press
27500 Drake Rd.
Farmington Hills, MI 48331-3535
Or you can visit our Internet site at gale.cengage.com

For product information and technology assistance, contact us at

Gale Customer Support, 1-800-877-4253
For permission to use material from this text or product, submit all requests online at www.cengage.com/permissions

Further permissions questions can be emailed to permissionrequest@cengage.com

Articles in Greenhaven Press anthologies are often edited for length to meet page requirements. In addition, original titles of these works are changed to clearly present the main thesis and to explicitly indicate the author's opinion. Every effort is made to ensure that Greenhaven Press accurately reflects the original intent of the authors. Every effort has been made to trace the owners of copyrighted material.

Cover photographs reproduced by permission of StuartWestmorland/Stone/Getty Images and Elnur/Dreamstime.com.

LIBRARY OF CONGRESS CATALOGING-IN-PUBLICATION DATA

Endangered oceans / Louise I. Gerdes, book editor.
    p. cm. -- (Opposing viewpoints)
    Includes bibliographical references and index.
    ISBN-13: 978-0-7377-4210-7 (hardcover)
    ISBN-13: 978-0-7377-4211-4 (pbk.)
    1. Marine resources conservation. 2. Marine pollution. 3. Ocean--Environmental aspects. I. Gerdes, Louise I., 1953-
    GC1018.E528 2009
    333.95'616--dc22

                                                        2008036462

Printed in the United States of America
1 2 3 4 5 6 7 12 11 10 09 08

3 1000 00036 2296

Contents

Chapter 2: What Ocean Policies Are Best?

Chapter 3: What Strategies Would Best Promote Sustainable Fishing?

Chapter 4: What Impact Do Human Activities Have on Marine Mammals?

Why Consider
Opposing Viewpoints?

"*The only way in which a human being can make some approach to knowing the whole of a subject is by hearing what can be said about it by persons of every variety of opinion and studying all modes in which it can be looked at by every character of mind. No wise man ever acquired his wisdom in any mode but this.*"

John Stuart Mill

In our media-intensive culture it is not difficult to find differing opinions. Thousands of newspapers and magazines and dozens of radio and television talk shows resound with differing points of view. The difficulty lies in deciding which opinion to agree with and which "experts" seem the most credible. The more inundated we become with differing opinions and claims, the more essential it is to hone critical reading and thinking skills to evaluate these ideas. *Opposing Viewpoints* books address this problem directly by presenting stimulating debates that can be used to enhance and teach these skills. The varied opinions contained in each book examine many different aspects of a single issue. While examining these conveniently edited opposing views, readers can develop critical thinking skills such as the ability to compare and contrast authors' credibility, facts, argumentation styles, use of persuasive techniques, and other stylistic tools. In short, the *Opposing Viewpoints* Series is an ideal way to attain the higher-level thinking and reading skills so essential in a culture of diverse and contradictory opinions.

In addition to providing a tool for critical thinking, Opposing Viewpoints books challenge readers to question their own strongly held opinions and assumptions. Most people form their opinions on the basis of upbringing, peer pressure, and personal, cultural, or professional bias. By reading carefully balanced opposing views, readers must directly confront new ideas as well as the opinions of those with whom they disagree. This is not to simplistically argue that everyone who reads opposing views will—or should—change his or her opinion. Instead, the series enhances readers' understanding of their own views by encouraging confrontation with opposing ideas. Careful examination of others' views can lead to the readers' understanding of the logical inconsistencies in their own opinions, perspective on why they hold an opinion, and the consideration of the possibility that their opinion requires further evaluation.

Evaluating Other Opinions

To ensure that this type of examination occurs, *Opposing Viewpoints* books present all types of opinions. Prominent spokespeople on different sides of each issue as well as well-known professionals from many disciplines challenge the reader. An additional goal of the series is to provide a forum for other, less known, or even unpopular viewpoints. The opinion of an ordinary person who has had to make the decision to cut off life support from a terminally ill relative, for example, may be just as valuable and provide just as much insight as a medical ethicist's professional opinion. The editors have two additional purposes in including these less known views. One, the editors encourage readers to respect others' opinions—even when not enhanced by professional credibility. It is only by reading or listening to and objectively evaluating others' ideas that one can determine whether they are worthy of consideration. Two, the inclusion of such viewpoints encourages the important critical thinking skill of objectively evaluating an author's credentials and bias. This evaluation will illuminate an author's reasons for taking a particular stance on an issue and will aid in readers' evaluation of the author's ideas.

It is our hope that these books will give readers a deeper understanding of the issues debated and an appreciation of the complexity of even seemingly simple issues when good and honest people disagree. This awareness is particularly important in a democratic society such as ours in which people enter into public debate to determine the common good. Those with whom one disagrees should not be regarded as enemies but rather as people whose views deserve careful examination and may shed light on one's own.

Thomas Jefferson once said that "difference of opinion leads to inquiry, and inquiry to truth." Jefferson, a broadly educated man, argued that "if a nation expects to be ignorant and free . . . it expects what never was and never will be." As individuals and as a nation, it is imperative that we consider the opinions of others and examine them with skill and discernment. The *Opposing Viewpoints* Series is intended to help readers achieve this goal.

David L. Bender and Bruno Leone,
Founders

Introduction

"It's a big ocean out there, and everybody assumes it can take care of itself."
—Leon Panetta,
Chairman, Pew Oceans Commission.

The oceans endow Americans with an enormous bounty. They provide its citizens with food, breathtaking views, and places to swim and surf. America's coasts are home to many and places to escape for those who vacation there. While coastal communities make up only 17 percent of U.S. land area, they are home to more than 50 percent of the nation's population, and more and more Americans migrate to the coasts each year. "Ocean-related activities add $4.5 trillion to the U.S. gross national product and account for 60 million jobs. America's 4.5 million square miles of coastal and marine waters are an economic paradise," claims policy analyst Beth Dickey. However, as she suggests, "there's trouble in paradise."

The stress of the human coastal invasion threatens ocean resources. Marine species are declining and fisheries are collapsing. Pollutants flow freely into coastal waters. "Swimmers are turned away from sewage-soaked beaches. Seafood is served up with a warning that eating it can make you sick," Dickey cautions. Nevertheless, little has been done to prevent marine pollution, coastal erosion, habitat loss, and fishery failures. Some wonder why the problems facing the nation's ocean resources have gone so long ignored. For many Americans, the oceans remain out of sight and out of mind. The environmental deterioration of the nation's ocean resources "would never be allowed to get that far on land," reasons U.S. congressman Sam Farr of California. While people readily recognize the dangers of smog-choked skies and the ravages of clear-cut forests, threats to the ocean are largely invisible—the problems facing the oceans often go unseen. When marine scientists began to sound the alarm, the public concern that might have led to significant political action failed to materialize.

During the 1980s, some in Congress, particularly those who represent coastal communities, did heed the warnings and worked persistently to stir the government to action. However, it took two decades to do so. In 2000, Congress established the U.S. Commission on Ocean Policy (USCOP). Four years later the commission issued its report—one year after a similar report prepared by the Pew Oceans Commission. Both reports not only urged a prompt response to the serious threats facing the nation's ocean resources but also blamed the confusing government bureaucracy that was created to protect these resources. According to USCOP chairman, James D. Watkins, "Our failures to properly manage the human activities that affect the nation's oceans, coasts and Great Lakes is compromising their ecological integrity, diminishing our ability to fully realize their potential, costing us jobs and revenue, threatening human health, and putting our future at risk." The Pew report lamented the "hodgepodge of ocean laws and programs," claiming that they lacked teeth or clear, measurable goals. "Plagued with systematic problems," the Pew report maintains, "U.S. ocean governance is in disarray." Indeed, America's waters are managed under 140 different laws spread across twenty different government agencies. Both reports agreed that America's oceans and fisheries are "in serious trouble" and both called for strong federal leadership. "We can't wait until we have the 9/11 of the oceans, and then do the investigation," claims Watkins.

In the years following these reports, Congress proposed numerous bills, but few led to any significant changes in ocean policy. Managing marine resources is indeed a challenge. Marine ecosystems are complex and linked to other ecosystems by broad spans of water and species movement. One strategy to address the problem of uncoordinated, piecemeal approaches to protecting marine species and habitats has been the creation of a network of marine protected areas (MPAs). The MPA networks link different marine habitats to help meet the biological needs of multiple species throughout their life stages. However, this solution was not appropriate for all species, particularly migratory species. Moreover, MPAs did not address factors other than fishing, such as pollution, tourism, and development, which also stress marine habitats. Recently, marine researchers have begun to recommend an even broader, system-wide approach to marine management known as ecosystem-based management (EBM). For EBM to work, however, would require unity among many government agencies and strong leadership.

Many hope that the most recent ocean bill will do just that. In June 2007 California's Farr introduced H.R. 21, the Ocean Conservation, Education, and National Strategy for the 21st Century Act (OCEANS 21). The primary goals of the act are to unify management under a national oceans' policy and streamline federal oversight and decision making by strengthening the National Oceanic and Atmospheric Administration. OCEANS 21 would also put in place an EBM plan to solve regional problems. "OCEANS 21 establishes a national policy to protect, maintain and restore the health of our marine ecosystems. It creates a process by which federal, state and local government agencies can better coordinate their activities to achieve goals and milestones for improving ocean health," claims Chris Mann of the Pew Environment Group. "This bill also gives the National Oceanic and Atmospheric Administration, for the first time, a clear, statutory mission to carry out ocean observation, research, and conservation," Mann maintains.

The act is not without its critics. Some fear that the new legislation will simply create an unnecessary, redundant bureaucracy that will conflict with existing marine management.

"Instead of enhancing the effectiveness and efficiency of our nation's ocean management regimes," claims the Marine Conservation Alliance's executive director David Benton, "HR 21 further complicates the array of laws, regulations and policies that currently govern ocean uses." Skeptics also question the effectiveness of untested EBM practices that may thwart current efforts to improve marine conservation. According to Benton, "Blind adherence, or in this case a legal requirement, to act on poor information is not, in our opinion, good resource management."

The OCEANS 21 debate is reflective of many controversies in the dispute over the problems facing the world's oceans and how best to address these concerns. Because marine ecosystems and the human interests that depend on them are complex, policies that protect marine habitats are hotly contested, often creating political paralysis. In the meantime, the stress on the world's oceans continues. Sarah Chasis, Ocean Initiative Director for the Natural Resources Defense Council, pleads, "Our oceans are in a state of silent collapse and we need our government to act now in order to reverse this trend. The longer we wait to address problems like pollution, habitat degradation and overexploitation, the harder and more expensive it will be to fix them." Whether OCEANS 21 will address her concerns remains to be seen. The authors of the viewpoints in *Opposing Viewpoints: Endangered Oceans* debate similar issues concerning the nature and scope of the problems facing the world's oceans and how best to protect them in the following chapters: What Threatens the World's Oceans? What Ocean Policies Are Best? What Strategies Would Best Promote Sustainable Fishing? What Impact Do Human Activities Have on Marine Mammals?

What Threatens the World's Oceans?

Chapter Preface

In the documentary *An Inconvenient Truth*, Al Gore warns of a twenty-foot rise in sea levels by 2010. *U.S. News & World Report* maintains that by mid-century "the chic Art Deco hotels that now line Miami's South Beach could stand waterlogged and abandoned." Environmental skeptic Bjorn Lomborg claims, however, that little reliable science backs up such claims. Sea levels, he asserts, have risen "no more than the change we have experienced since 1940 and less than the change those Art Deco hotels have already stood through." The dispute over rising sea levels is one of the enduring controversies of the global warming debate, and those who contest the threats facing the world's oceans have joined the fray. While some claim that rising sea levels will ravage coastal marine environments and the communities that depend on them, others assert that such claims are simply environmentalist hysteria.

Many scientists believe that rising sea levels will have a devastating impact on the wetland ecosystems that serve as a bridge between the oceans and coastal communities. Wetlands filter and cleanse drinking water, retain floodwater, harbor freshwater fish and shellfish, and serve as nurseries for many forms of marine life. According to the Union of Concerned Scientists (UCS), a twenty-inch rise in sea level could reduce coastal wetlands in the United States by almost half. As a result, barrier islands and port cities will be at greater risk of flooding and erosion. "Salt water will intrude into estuaries and aquifers, harming wetland species and compromising water supplies," UCS explains. Because of rising sea levels, these scientists assert, many who inhabit the world's highly populated coastal regions will suffer tremendous economic and social upheaval. While the United States, as a developed nation, can spend billions of dollars hoping to prevent flooding and protect its water supply, the world's poorer nations cannot afford these protections, and millions will be displaced, UCS predicts.

While few now dispute the reality of global warming, some argue that the threats posed are exaggerated, including the risks of rising sea levels. "People have been given the impression that the 18 cm sea level rise claimed for the 20th century is an observed quantity.... It is not," claims John L. Daly of the Greening Earth Society. Skeptics assert that computer model predictions of sea-level rise are not backed up by empirical evidence. According to geodynamics scholar Nils-Axel Morner, satellite measures have shown no significant changes in sea level. "This implies that there is no fear of any massive future flooding as claimed in most global warming scenarios," Morner maintains. The rise in sea level, critics contend, is rather a shift in the amount of water from one area to another area of the globe. Moreover, skeptics suggest, global warming hysteria does not promote productive policy. Lomborg recommends that commentators should "rein in the exaggerations, and start focusing on where we can do the most good."

Whether sea levels are indeed rising, posing a serious threat to wetlands and the coastal communities they support, remains hotly contested. The authors in the following chapter present their views in answer to the question, what threatens the world's oceans?

> *"The activities of humanity . . . are having a huge and distinctly bad impact on the world's oceans."*

Human Activities Threaten the World's Oceans

Bahá'í International Community

Human activities threaten the oceans on which human survival depends, claims the Bahá'í International Community (BIC) in the following viewpoint. Overfishing, the authors assert, for example, has depleted the numbers of many fish species that provide food and jobs for millions. According to the BIC, only policies that recognize all people as one human family with a shared responsibility to respect the world's oceans will protect the bounty the oceans provide. BIC is a nongovernmental organization that represents the members of the Bahá'í faith.

As you read, consider the following questions:

1. According to the BIC, what is the predominant feature of the earth and the predominant form of life?
2. In the authors' opinion, what economic benefits come from the world's oceans?
3. How does the BIC define sustainable development?

Bahá'í International Community, "Perspectives: The Blue Planet: Oceans in Crisis," *One Country*, April–June 2006. Reproduced by permission.

The astronauts of Apollo 8, on the first mission around the moon in 1968, took a now famous photograph. Called "Earthrise," it shows the grey and lifeless horizon of the moon—and suspended above it, against the infinite blackness of space, is our bright and blue home planet.

Along with other images from space, that photograph has had a huge impact on humanity's collective consciousness. It offered an undeniable vision of our interdependence, proof that we all share a single home, with nowhere else to go should we irreparably damage this one.

The photograph also revealed another fact: the predominant color of our planet is blue. That's because, of course, more than 70 percent of its surface is covered by water. Oceans, not land, are the predominant feature of the earth, and sea creatures the predominant form of life.

Taking the Oceans for Granted

Despite this fact, or perhaps because of it, land-dwelling humanity has by and large taken the world's oceans for granted. Viewed through a traditional mind-set that held that their wealth was free for the taking, the oceans were long seen as a bottomless supply of fish, seafood and other natural resources—and also a nearly infinite waste dump.

It now appears that humanity's heedlessness may soon catch up with it.

A series of recent reports and studies indicates that the oceans are on the verge of a crisis. They include the 2003 Pew Oceans Commission, the 2004 Status of Coral Reefs of the World report, and the 2005 Millennium Ecosystem Assessment by the United Nations Environment Programme (UNEP).

Within this body of research, there is a common theme: that the activities of humanity—fishing, farming, development, industrial processes, and consumerism—are having a huge and distinctly bad impact on the world's oceans. Moreover, this impact is going largely unnoticed and undiscussed.

Humanity's collective prosperity and long-term prospects for survival are intimately linked to the health of the world's oceans. To cite just a few key points: fishing provides some 12 percent of the world's food supply, photosynthesis in the oceans provides about half of the world's oxygen replenishment, and the oceans play a crucial role in moderating the global climate.

The economic benefits derived from the oceans are huge, as well. Fishing and fish products provide direct employment to some 38 million people and an estimated $124 billion in economic benefits. The oceans provide an essential transportation link for global trade, not to mention their recreational value. Oceans also provide a resource for petroleum and scarce minerals.

The Price of Collective Neglect

Our collective neglect of the world's oceans, however, puts much of this at risk. Among the urgent problems facing the oceans are:

- *Overfishing.* Recent studies indicated that the number of fish species has declined by 50 percent in the last 50 years—and that the populations of large fish, those species that have traditionally been sought by fishermen, have declined by 90 percent over the same time period. Specialists blame the rise of high-tech, industrial-scale fishing fleets that use sonar, satellite data, and other systems to track schools of fish to their most remote habitats for much of this problem.

- *Pollution.* While oil-spills and toxic substances like mercury and PBBs [polybromobiphenyls] have perhaps been uppermost in the public's mind when they think of ocean pollution, a far larger problem is emerging as

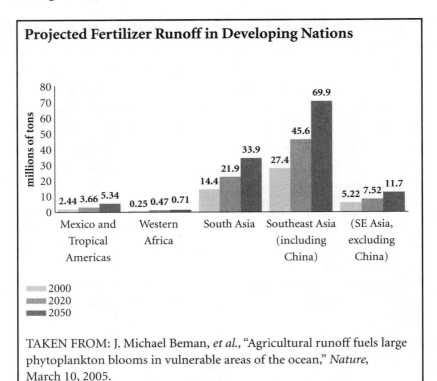

Projected Fertilizer Runoff in Developing Nations

millions of tons

| Mexico and Tropical Americas | Western Africa | South Asia | Southeast Asia (including China) | (SE Asia, excluding China) |

2.44 3.66 5.34 — 0.25 0.47 0.71 — 14.4 21.9 33.9 — 27.4 45.6 69.9 — 5.22 7.52 11.7

2000
2020
2050

TAKEN FROM: J. Michael Beman, *et al.*, "Agricultural runoff fuels large phytoplankton blooms in vulnerable areas of the ocean," *Nature*, March 10, 2005.

excess fertilizer runs off from farms and fields into the world's rivers. The nutrients in fertilizers, as well as sewage run-offs, are causing a wide variety of problems, from toxic algae blooms that overwhelm other sea life to the proliferation of harmful bacteria.

- *Acidification.* Excess carbon dioxide, a by-product of fossil fuel use that threatens to change the atmosphere's average temperature, is also finding its way into the oceans. And when water absorbs excess carbon dioxide, it turns acidic—an effect that scientists are beginning to link to further declines in fish and other sea creatures. By the end of the century, according to a report in the *Los Angeles Times*, ocean acidity is expected to be two-and-a-half times what it was before the Industrial Revolution. "Such a change would devastate many species of fish and other animals that have thrived in chemically stable seawater for millions of years," the *Times* reported.

- *Plastics.* The accumulation of cast-off garbage—and particularly plastic garbage—is killing off seabirds and ocean wildlife at increasingly higher rates. By one count, nearly 90% of floating marine litter is composed of plastic, which when ingested by sea creatures often slowly strangles or starves them. Such plastic litter does not degrade, and it can be expected to last in the ocean for hundreds of years.

A Shared Responsibility

There is an increasing awareness of the scope, scale and interconnectedness of these threats—and the degree to which they threaten both humanity's near future and long-term prosperity.

"Humankind has used and exploited the ocean's resources extensively and sometimes destructively," said the International Council of Academies of Engineering and Technological Sciences in a July 2005 statement. "Through the interconnectedness of the ocean's physical, geological and ecological systems, we all ultimately bear the consequences, good or bad. There is thus an inescapable international responsibility for what happens in and to the ocean."

This shared international responsibility is recognized in a limited way in such agreements as the Convention on the Law of the Sea, which sets out rights regarding navigation, territorial sea limits, economic jurisdiction, seabed resources, and the passage of ships through narrow straits, as well as on the conservation and management of living marine resources and the protection of the marine environment.

Yet, as can easily be inferred from the list of threats to the ocean, the Convention does not go far enough in protecting one of the planet's greatest resources, not for now, not for future generations.

Part of the problem is that there are many competing interests—from nation-states to corporations to individual fishermen, farmers and sailors. And there is much at stake—from wholesale questions about the use of fertilizers, which are currently so important to land-based food production, to issues of biodiversity related to the extinction of aquatic life. So it is hard to envision from where and how the impetus for international cooperation and coordinated action will come.

All of these issues also properly fall under the rubric of sustainable development, which is of course the generalized term for the emerging paradigm that seeks to balance such varied issues as development, environmental conservation, consumption, human rights, population, and justice.

The Oneness of Humanity

For Bahá'ís, the answer to balancing such competing concerns, whether for the oceans or sustainable development in general, lies in achieving a better understanding of the spiritual principles and realities behind human existence. Foremost among the new spiritual principles for this age is the oneness of humanity.

"Ye are the fruits of one tree, and the leaves of one branch," wrote Bahá'u'lláh. "The earth is but one country, and mankind its citizens."

In numerous statements, the Bahá'í International Community has long underscored the importance of this principle in any vision of sustainable development. "Only when individuals see themselves as members of one human family, sharing one common homeland, will they be able to commit themselves to the far-reaching changes, on the individual and collective levels, which an increasingly interdependent and rapidly changing world mandates," said the Community in a statement in 1992 in the lead-up to the Earth Summit.

Moreover, the Bahá'í writings ultimately anticipate the creation of a world federal system with a representative world parliament "whose members will, as the trustees of the whole of mankind, ultimately control the entire resources of all the component nations, and will enact such laws as shall be required to regulate the life, satisfy the needs and adjust the relationships of all races and people."

Humanity is beginning to awaken to the collective damage that is being done to the oceans of the world. Humanity is also coming to understand that our oceans are part of the global commons—something that must be held in trust for future generations. What's needed now is a comprehensive recognition of our underlying interdependence and essential oneness. Only that can provide the insight and motivating force to bring about the kinds of changes in our laws, lifestyles, and consciousness that will be necessary both to protect the oceans and draw on their wealth in a way that benefits all humanity.

It's worth reconsidering the Earthrise photograph taken by astronauts nearly 40 years ago. The earth is one—and blue. These facts are fundamentally interlinked.

"Ocean conservationists [should] focus on a single message, one that combines the seriousness of the threat with optimism that it can be overcome."

The Threat to the World's Oceans Can Be Overcome

Jack Sterne and David Wilmot

Although the world's oceans are in a state of decline, problems such as overfishing and pollution can be overcome, argue Jack Sterne and David Wilmot in the following viewpoint. The problems facing the oceans are largely invisible to the public because people cannot easily see the damage done, the authors maintain; however, they claim, growing grassroots efforts led by a broad base of those who use the ocean can increase awareness and overcome the lack of political will that has so far led to poor ocean policies. Sterne and Wilmot are cofounders of Ocean Champions, a political action organization.

As you read, consider the following questions:

1. What three reasons do Sterne and Wilmot give for a lack of leadership on ocean policy issues?

2. According to the authors, what mistake did ocean conservationists make for many years?

3. In the authors' opinion, what message must ocean conservationists focus on in order to lead a successful campaign?

In its March/April [2006] issue, *Mother Jones* presents a dire, often depressing, but sadly accurate assessment of the state of the world's oceans. To many, these issues are brand new, as the crisis in the oceans has largely been "out of sight, out of mind" to date. In reality, the problems afflicting the ocean—too much fishing, too much pollution, and a broken management system—have been with us for years, but little has been done about them.

And while the pace of decline has unquestionably accelerated recently, the real question raised by this series of articles is: "Where is the leadership?" Most environmental groups have been focused largely on terrestrial issues, Congress is missing in action, and the public's attention is elsewhere (usually on the latest episode of "Survivor" or "Lost," which is where we might all end up if we don't reverse current trends).

What does it say that, though we literally "carry the oceans within ourselves," and though we are so drawn to it that over half the U.S. population lives in a coastal county, our oceans languish in neglect, while the biggest environmental fight of our time is over oil drilling in a patch of Arctic wilderness that most people will never visit, and that has a fraction of the ecological significance of our oceans?

Activists Without Power

In a 2003 report for the Packard, Oak and Munson Foundations, [Ocean Champions] looked in detail at the effectiveness of the ocean conservation movement. We found a growing force of highly professional activists pressing for essential reforms but not yet able to muster the political power to achieve

Advances in Scientific Understanding

There are two key areas where scientific understanding has advanced considerably since biodiversity loss became widely recognized as a global problem. . . . First, we are considerably more aware of the inherent and functional losses that occur with species extinction and loss of biodiversity. Second, there is also increased understanding of the interdependence of health across the diverse species and systems within the biosphere—providing the impetus for a "one health" perspective that bridges human, wildlife, and ecosystem health.

Bruce A. Wilcox and A. Alonso Aguirre,
EcoHealth, *2004.*

victory. While the oceans have bipartisan support in Congress, there are very few champions willing to expend political capital to bring about the needed reforms.

The problem is not a dearth of good facts or the lack of a compelling scientific case. (If you think that an overwhelming scientific consensus is enough to win, look at Congress' inaction on global warming.) Rather, it has been the conspicuous absence of ocean conservationists from the political arena, and the lack of an effective grassroots base that can be mobilized to pressure politicians for change. The result: extremely limited leverage to reward those politicians who will work to protect the ocean or to hold accountable those who would destroy it.

In part, the fault lies with ocean conservationists ourselves; we have failed to capture the public's attention on the issues. Not that doing so is easy. Although so much of the population lives near and/or recreates at the ocean, the problems of the ocean are largely abstract and invisible; we can't *see* what bottom-trawling does to the floor of the ocean the way we can see what clear-cutting does to a mountainside.

Despite what seems to us a compelling message (an ocean largely devoid of magnificent creatures like marlin, sea turtles, and sharks, replaced by little more than jellyfish) public urgency on this issue is not there. Somewhere there is a breakdown in the "educate, motivate, and activate" sequence.

All Is Not Lost

But all is not lost. We believe there is a latent "grassroots" base of ocean users comprising recreational fishermen, divers, surfers, and sailors, among others. The Marine Fish Conservation Network, for instance, has built an effective coalition of environmentalists and recreational and commercial fishermen to advocate for fisheries reform. And groups like the Surfrider Foundation are turning surfers into activists.

On the political level, for all the challenges, there is cause for optimism, too. Ocean conservationists for many years made the mistake of many people of conscience, believing that involvement in electoral politics was somehow dirty or unethical, and that simply arming political leaders with the "facts" would lead to positive change. If we care about an issue like the oceans, to be successful we must be willing to work to get good people elected and to hold accountable those who are not. That is beginning to change.

The politics of the ocean are often very different from other environmental issues. On the one hand, the oceans have a few tireless champions like Rep. Sam Farr (D-Ca.) who represents the Monterey Bay area. But consider that Rep. Barney Frank (D-Mass.), with generally one of the best environmental voting records in Congress, has been leading the fight against tough overfishing regulations in federal law, largely because he has an active concentration of commercial fishermen in his district who could place his re-election in jeopardy if he is not responsive to their demands, however short-sighted they may be. And the senator who has shown the most leadership on fisheries policy is Sen. Ted Stevens (R-AK), better known for his efforts to open [to oil exploration the] ANWR [Arctic National Wildlife Refuge].

Building Political Power

To help ocean conservationists build political power, in 2003 we launched the first political organizations for the oceans, Ocean Champions and Ocean Champions Voter Fund, to help politicians who care about the oceans get elected to Congress (and to defeat bad ones, like [former California] Rep. Richard Pombo and to "brand" oceans as a political issue. Our early efforts have been promising. For instance, Ocean Champions endorsed and supported 14 candidates in 2004; 11 were elected, including two brand-new members of Congress (one Republican and one Democrat) who are already taking a leadership role in pushing for positive fisheries legislation and opposing efforts to open up our oceans and coasts to new drilling for oil and gas. . . .

Time is short. More resources must be directed by both national and grassroots organizations to the task of awakening the public. This is an issue that should be even more compelling to the public than global warming, if only because so much of the public recreates at the ocean. It will require an unprecedented public relations campaign, far outstripping anything that has gone before it.

Such a successful campaign is going to require ocean conservationists to focus on a single message, one that combines the seriousness of the threat with optimism that it can be overcome. That message must be delivered by credible messengers over and over again until the public demands action.

Are we willing to create the kind of sustained and strategic campaign that persuades the public and our political leaders that this is a crisis that threatens our future as a species? Are we also willing to invest in electoral politics, to help elect members of both parties who will fight for the oceans? These questions must be asked, and they must be answered. It's a matter of leadership.

> *"A fifth of the reefs . . . have been de-*
> *stroyed and are not recovering. Another*
> *quarter face the threat of imminent col-*
> *lapse from human activities."*

Loss of Coral Reefs Threatens the World's Oceans

Peter N. Spotts

In the following viewpoint, Peter N. Spotts argues that a fifth of the world's coral reefs are already destroyed, and the rest are in danger because of overfishing, soil and nutrient runoff, carbon dioxide emissions, and climate change. Spotts notes what scientists are doing to try to recover the coral reefs from the virtually back-to-back bleaching events of the summers of 1998 to 2002, due to climate change and explains the importance of reef conservation and protection. He urges that action must be taken now to save them. Peter N. Spotts is a staff writer at The Christian Science Monitor.

As you read, consider the following questions:

1. How many miles long is the Great Barrier Reef, according to Spotts?

Peter N. Spotts, "The Struggle to Save Earth's Largest Life Form," *Christian Science Monitor*, March 10, 2005. Copyright © 2005 The Christian Science Publishing Society. All rights reserved. Reproduced by permission from *Christian Science Monitor* (www.csmonitor.com).

2. What causes coral bleaching events, in the author's opinion?

3. According to Spotts, what percentage of the Great Barrier Reef is now a no-take zone?

Leaf through the latest tomes on the status of coral reefs worldwide and a grim picture emerges. Because of overfishing, soil and nutrient runoff from land, and climate change:

- A fifth of the reefs—among the planet's most productive habitats—have been destroyed and are not recovering.

- Another quarter face the threat of imminent collapse from human activities.

- Another quarter are said to face long-term collapse.

Preserving Resilience

"If we've learned anything in the last 10 years, it's how to kill a coral reef," says coral ecologist Terry Hughes ruefully.

Those dire facts, drawn from the latest "Global Coral Reef Status Report," however, are serving as a springboard for devising strategies to save the world's coral communities and, by extension, the thousands of marine species that rely on them. The best way to do this, many marine ecologists now maintain, is to focus on a reef's ability to bounce back from hardship. Where ecologists once talked about saving species, habitats, and biodiversity in a tropical reef ecosystem, many now speak of preserving "resilience."

Nowhere is this approach to reef conservation being put through its paces more rigorously than along Australia's Great Barrier Reef [GBR]—dubbed by some the largest living thing on Earth. In fact, the GBR is a chain of 2,900 reefs stretching some 1,200 miles along Australia's east coast. Slowly expanding its reach as sea levels have risen following the last ice age, the network covers just over 135,000 square miles of coastal ocean.

Beyond its immediate biological value, the reef system represents a ringing cash register for the state of Queensland. Tourism and related activities bring in roughly $1.2 billion (Australian; US$950 million) a year to the region. The reef network also serves as a buffer between the mainland and the high seas that accompany tropical cyclones.

In the past, researchers would study tropical-reef response to single events—such as a hurricane, tropical cyclone, or coral bleaching—to evaluate its ability to bounce back.

"People wrote about these as one-off events," explains Dr. Hughes, a professor at James Cook University in Townsville. "But on longer time frames—from decades to centuries—those are recurrent events. We're now asking: How can this system, on a scale of thousands of kilometers, absorb recurring disturbances without going belly-up? Resilience is about the system absorbing changes" and conservation managers "being proactive in anticipating them."

Climate Change

Calls for this broader approach have been heard for some time. But the need was driven home by virtually back-to-back coral-bleaching events in the summers of 1998 and 2002, during which coastal waters grew unusually warm. Under conditions of high heat and light, the algae that lived in the coral, provided it with food, and gave it its distinctive color, underwent a Jekyll-and-Hyde change. The algae became corrosive, eating away at the coral from the inside. In self-defense, the coral expelled the algae—and with it the coral's source of food. The coral turned white and died.

Both bleaching events involved vast tracts of coral, with 2002's event marked as the worst bleaching event on record along the GBR. To many scientists here, these were harbingers

The Risks of Coral Reef Loss

Loss of coral reefs ... mean not only changes to treasured ecosystems harbouring vast amounts of biodiversity, but also the loss of ecosystem services that serve and protect human communities. Tourism and recreational use of tropical areas will decline as reefs are degraded, as carbonate sands formed by reef ecosystem processes dwindle, and as reefs become less diverse and monochromatic.

We are, however, not talking only of ruining the vacation plans of wealthy tourists. Many coastal economies are wholly dependent on coastal tourism and marine resources. Moreover, coral reefs provide a major source of food for a large part of the global population, and they provide coastlines and communities important buffering from storms and tsunamis. If reefs stop growing and cannot keep pace with rising sea levels, these important ecosystem services will be lost.

Tundi Agardi, Fish Information & Services, April 21, 2007.

of the future as Earth's climate warms—at least in part because of carbon dioxide rising into the atmosphere as humans burn coal, oil, and other fossil fuels.

"Climate change is no longer a future issue for Australians—it's happening," Hughes says.

Even modest sea-surface warming, say 1 or 2 degrees C—the midrange forecast of the Intergovernmental Panel on Climate Change—could prompt large declines in coral communities by 2050, according to Ray Berkelmans and colleagues at the Australian Institute of Marine Science (AIMS) and the US National Oceanic and Atmospheric Administration in a study [in 2004].

The concern: As global warming heats the ocean surface, bleaching events will happen more often, giving reefs less time to recover—all other things being equal, Dr. Berkelmans and others say. Added to that stress, they say, is the destruction that would come from tropical cyclones, which are expected to grow more intense, if not more frequent, as global warming proceeds.

One potential offset to bleaching could be coral's potential for adapting to warmer waters. Some coral communities have been able to survive warmer waters by embracing algae that are more tolerant of heat than their previous tenants, according to a team of scientists led by Andrew Baker, a researcher with the Center for Environmental Research and Conservation at Columbia University in New York. Their findings were reported in the journal *Nature* [in August 2004].

But there may be limits to how broadly these results apply, others say. Even without pressure from climate change, reefs also face pressure from overfishing, farm and ranch runoff, and soil erosion.

Reef Conservation

[In July 2004], after several years of debate and negotiation, Australia's federal government took a significant step by declaring fully one-third of the reef a no-take zone—no fishing, capturing live fish, or collecting corals. Previously, no-take areas covered only about 5 percent of the reef.

At the same time, the state of Queensland adopted a program for reducing the silt and nutrients that flow onto the reef from rivers in the region. The silt can cut light and smother young coral before they can replenish a bleached area. The nutrients can lead to explosions of algae and Crown of Thorns starfish, which can turn healthy reefs into drab undersea barrens.

Having figured out the historical impact of silt from rivers, an AIMS team is embarking on a five-year project to pin down more precisely the biological effects of the nutrients and soil across broader reaches of the reef system.

As these scientists head to the reef to get a better handle on the factors that determine the GBR's resilience, others are using those data to build models to forecast resilience.

For example, Scott Wooldridge is developing a "state of the reef" computer model at AIMS that will allow conservation managers to rank the resilience potential for different reefs or reef segments. The model has the potential for use worldwide. So far, he's included three elements: adequate levels of grazing fish on the reef to keep algae at bay, water quality, and increased heat-tolerance among coral—which he acknowledges is the weakest link in the chain in terms of biological research.

The model points to some disturbing results. Australia—and specifically, the Great Barrier Reef Marine Park Authority—may have chosen the wrong approach when it set up its no-take areas, he says.

His preliminary results suggest that the northern third of the reef probably should get the most conservation attention. The park agency, by contrast, set aside ecologically representative areas scattered throughout the reef. That made sense at the time, Dr. Wooldridge says, given what scientists then knew. But the northern segment is more pristine and faces fewer stresses because fewer people live and visit there. While it will likely feel the bleaching effects of climate change more strongly at first than reef sections farther south, it still stands a good chance of surviving. Thus it will be able to provide the larvae that will ride prevailing currents south to reseed portions of the reef that are under greater multiple stresses.

It's a controversial notion, Wooldridge acknowledges, and calls into question the strategy over which the government spent so much time and political capital.

"With proper management, you can still have a viable reef by 2050," he says. "But the implications are that we need to conserve more in the north."

"Research has significantly expanded the
understanding of processes affecting the
structure, function, and health of coral
reef ecosystems."

Efforts to Protect the World's Coral Reefs Are Progressing

Timothy R.E. Keeney

*In the following viewpoint, Timothy R.E. Keeney maintains that
U.S. agencies such as the National Oceanic and Atmospheric
Administration (NOAA), in collaboration with worldwide coral
reef protection organizations, have taken significant steps to protect coral reefs. NOAA research, Keeney contends, has increased
understanding of the processes that impact the health of coral
reef ecosystems and, therefore, the policies that will best protect
them. These agencies also increase public awareness and teach
coastal communities how best to preserve local coral reefs, he
claims. Keeney is deputy assistant secretary for oceans and atmosphere at NOAA.*

As you read, consider the following questions:

1. According to Keeney, what are some of the benefits that
   coral reefs provide?

Timothy R.E. Keeney, "Hearing on the Coral Reef Conservation Act," in Subcommittee
on Fisheries and Oceans, Committee on Resources, U.S. House of Representatives,
March 1, 2005.

2. What discoveries have resulted from NOAA research, in the author's view?

3. In Keeney's opinion, how does NOAA play a role in international coral reef conservation?

Coral reefs, often called the "rainforests of the sea," are among the oldest and most diverse ecosystems on the planet. Coral reefs provide resources and services worth billions of dollars each year to the United States economy and economies worldwide, a surprising amount considering that these ecosystems cover less than one percent of the Earth's surface. Ten and a half million people in the United States live in coastal communities adjacent to coral reefs. Consequently, coral reefs have become an integral part of the culture, heritage, and economies of these regions. Coral reef resources provide economic and environmental benefits in the form of food, jobs, natural products, pharmaceuticals, and shoreline protection. In fact, the international media and South Asian officials have reported a dramatic reduction in deaths and destruction from the [2004] tsunami in some locations due to the wave-absorbing properties of healthy coral reef ecosystems. The Maldives, a nation considered among the most vulnerable to a tsunami, suffered far fewer deaths than some coastal areas of Sri Lanka and Indonesia as a result of the extensive coral reefs that encircle the islands.

Coral reef ecosystems have survived for millions of years despite an abundance of natural disturbances. Warming ocean temperatures and human-induced impacts, including pollution, overfishing, and physical damage are also having a significant effect on the health of coral reef ecosystems. A combination of stressors has caused a rapid decline in the health of many coral reefs globally and, if left unchecked, this decline could lead to significant social, economic, and environmental consequences. The Global Coral Reef Monitoring Network (GCRMN) estimates that 20 percent of the world's coral reefs have already been destroyed and predicts that 24 percent face impending destruction from adverse human impacts.

Addressing the Threats

Congress recognized the need to preserve, sustain, and restore the condition of coral reef ecosystems by passing the Coral Reef Conservation Act of 2000 (CRCA), calling for the creation of a national strategy and program to address the threats to coral reef communities. The CRCA calls for NOAA [National Oceanic and Atmospheric Administration] to carry out a number of activities to promote the wise management and sustainable use of coral reef ecosystems, to develop sound scientific information on the condition of coral reef ecosystems, and to assist in the preservation of coral reefs by supporting external conservation programs.

The CRCA established a national program to conduct activities to conserve coral reefs, which led to the creation of the NOAA Coral Reef Conservation Program (CRCP). The CRCP is a matrix program that draws experts together from throughout NOAA to develop integrated strategies to address coral reef decline. In addition, CRCP works with scientific, private, government and non-government partners to address coral reef conservation on local, national, and international scales.

One of NOAA's goals is to produce comprehensive digital maps of all shallow coral reefs (<30m) in the United States by 2009. Between 2002 and 2004, NOAA has been very active in our mapping efforts, with the percentage of shallow reef area mapped by NOAA increasing from 35 to 66 percent between 2002 and 2004. These habitat maps provide basic information about coral reef ecosystems to scientists and managers, assisting them in designing research and management plans, assessing damaged corals, monitoring reef health, and evaluating the results of their work.

Partnering with other federal agencies, as well as state and territorial governments, NOAA has helped build a national in-

Reef Rules for Snorkelers

- Take nothing living or dead out of the water except recent garbage.

- Never chase or try to ride marine life.

- Never touch, handle or feed marine life except under expert guidance and following local established guidelines.

- Avoid using gloves in coral environments.

Coral Reef Alliance, 2007.

tegrated coral reef monitoring system. Integrated monitoring programs measure and evaluate the condition of the ecosystem over time, help assess the efficacy of management actions, and provide comparable data sets and products that can be used to adapt these measures. In 2002, NOAA worked with federal, state, territorial and commonwealth partners to produce the first *State of Coral Reef Ecosystems of the United States and Pacific Freely Associated States.* This report assessed the condition of U.S. coral reefs, ranked threats in 13 geographic areas, detailed ongoing conservation actions taken by agencies participating in the U.S. Coral Reef Task Force (USCRTF), and provided recommendations from coral reef managers to fill information gaps. . . .

Expanding Understanding

NOAA-sponsored research has significantly expanded the understanding of processes affecting the structure, function, and health of coral reef ecosystems. This research provides managers with tools to improve the integrity and sustainable use of the Nation's coral reef ecosystems. For example, the Coral Disease and Health Consortium is coordinating scientific resources to investigate coral health, coral bleaching, and factors affecting the emergence, transmission, and impact of coral diseases, which are a major cause of reef degradation in Florida and the Caribbean.

NOAA research has resulted in the discovery of entirely new cold-water coral ecosystems, also known as deep-sea corals. These cold-water coral communities are most commonly found between 50 to 1000 meters in depth and are more broadly distributed than tropical coral reefs. Deep-sea corals occur on the edge of continental shelves and slopes throughout the U.S. exclusive economic zone. Research indicates that cold-water coral ecosystems, like tropical shallow-water corals, are potential "hot-spots" of marine biological diversity and function as important habitat for thousands of fish and invertebrate species. Additionally, cold-water corals are long-lived, slow-growing animals that are vulnerable to physical disturbances. The discovery of these characteristics has led to calls for enhanced conservation of these resources. NOAA is working with each of the Regional Fishery Management Councils (RFMC) to address the impacts that fishing efforts may have on these habitats, under the existing authority of the Magnuson-Stevens Fishery Management and Conservation Act. In February [2005], the North Pacific Fishery Management Council brokered a historic agreement between the environmental and the fishing communities in Alaska to protect approximately 290,000 square nautical miles in the Aleutian Islands and Gulf of Alaska from the impacts of mobile bottom-tending fishing gear; this area includes prime habitat for cold-water corals. Because most fishing in that region has historically occurred in the areas that would remain open, the economic impacts to fishing communities are minimal. . . .

NOAA's efforts under the CRCA have also addressed the threat to reefs from marine debris and abandoned vessels. Debris and vessels can cause physical harm to coral reefs, through entanglement and collision, and are serious concerns in some regions of the United States. Derelict fishing gear from distant water fisheries is the greatest anthropogenic impact to the coral reefs surrounding the Northwestern Hawaiian Islands (NWHI). NOAA leads a partnership with the State of Hawaii, Department of the Interior (DOI), U.S. Coast Guard, nongovernmental, and many local organizations to remove derelict fishing gear from the NWHI. Since 2001, this large-scale effort has removed over 400 metric tons of marine debris, and [in 2005] complete[d] removal of all major accumulations of debris from the NWHI. Because derelict fishing gear continues to accumulate in this area, NOAA and its partners have been coordinating an international discussion on this issue, and are conducting studies on how to detect and remove derelict fishing gear from the open ocean. NOAA has also created an Abandoned Vessels Program, which developed a comprehensive database of abandoned vessels used to identify candidate wrecks for further attention and to initiate removal of the highest priority cases.

Building Awareness

Outreach and education activities to build public awareness and local capacity are another way NOAA promotes sustainable management of coral reef ecosystems. NOAA has reached out to stakeholders both by creating and distributing educational materials and conducting workshops and training modules. For example, NOAA held a series of workshops with fishermen in Puerto Rico and the U.S. Virgin Islands to discuss community values and the importance of coral reefs to fishing livelihoods. NOAA has also assisted state and territorial governments in enhancing their human resource capacity for marine resource management by providing technical trainings and workshops for managers, by creating internship/fellowship programs, and by providing direct funding to support management staff. For example, NOAA funds Coral Management

Fellowships in six of the seven coral reef jurisdictions to assist states and territories with their conservation capacity needs. . . .

Creating Partnerships

NOAA, in collaboration with state and territory partners, has been conducting the first comprehensive, nationwide inventory and assessment of all U.S. coral reef–protected areas. This assessment is the first step in creating a national network of protected areas, which will help ensure the long-term viability, ecological integrity, and sustainable use of coral reefs. In addition, NOAA's National Marine Sanctuary Program conducts research and monitoring and promotes sound management within Fagatele Bay, Florida Keys, Flower Garden Banks, and Gray's Reef sanctuaries and the Northwest Hawaiian Islands Coral Reef Ecosystem Reserve.

NOAA plays a major role in international coral reef conservation. NOAA promotes improved human and institutional capacity to manage and conserve coral reefs internationally through technical assistance and its international coral small grants program. NOAA participates in multiple international efforts such as the International Coral Reef Initiative (ICRI), which supports international coral reef research and management efforts, and the Global Coral Reef Monitoring Network, which produces biennial *Status of Coral Reefs of the World* reports. The USCRTF and NOAA's partnership with the scientific community led to the U.S.'s successful bid to host the 2008 International Coral Reef Symposium, the largest international gathering of coral reef scientists and managers.

Finding Alternatives

NOAA continues to play an active role in the USCRTF. The Task Force was established by Executive Order and is composed of twelve federal agencies, seven states and territories, and the three freely associated states. As co-chair of the

USCRTF with DOI, NOAA leads the planning of the biannual USCRTF meetings. These meetings bring members together to discuss key issues, propose new actions, present progress reports, and update the coral community on past accomplishments and future plans. The USCRTF meetings provide a valuable venue for the exchange of information in which members can voice concerns about their coral reef conservation efforts and collaborate to find more effective alternatives. Many of NOAA's coral reef conservation efforts are the result of partnerships with the various federal agencies and state and territory governments on the USCRTF....

In 2002, NOAA, in cooperation with the USCRTF, published *A National Coral Reef Action Strategy* as required by the CRCA. The Strategy is based on the framework presented in the USCRTF's *National Action Plan*. The Strategy provides information on the major threats and needs in each jurisdiction and identifies priority actions needed to achieve the 13 goals and associated objectives defined in the Strategy. Two years after the Strategy was published and every two years thereafter, CRCA requires NOAA to submit a report describing all activities undertaken to implement the Strategy....

Supporting Continued Efforts

The authority provided to NOAA under the CRCA has provided many benefits to coral reef management and protection. The Administration recognized the importance of conserving corals in the U.S. Ocean Action Plan released on December 17, 2004. The President's 2006 budget request includes $27.199 million for the NOAA Coral Reef Conservation Program, including the $1.5 million in new funding to further implement local action strategies mentioned earlier. NOAA's continuing coral reef conservation efforts will include exploring designation of the Northwestern Hawaiian Islands Coral Reef Ecosystem Reserve as the 14⁰ National Marine Sanctuary; forming new international partnerships; re-establishing the interagency marine debris coordinating committee; fostering coral protection by recreational and agricultural interests; and developing criteria to evaluate the health of coral reefs and associated water quality.

Recent accomplishments represent only intermediate steps toward achieving the goals of the *National Coral Reef Action Strategy*. Much remains to be done to halt the degradation of coral reefs and to sustain these valuable marine ecosystems and the economies that depend on them. Reauthorization of the Coral Reef Conservation Act is an important step for continuing this work to protect and restore coral reefs in the United States and abroad. Reauthorization would allow continuation of important NOAA-sponsored research, the Coral Reef Conservation Fund partnership with NFWF [National Fish and Wildlife Foundation] (for which the authorities in the CRCA are needed).

> "Seabed-scouring trawlers and reckless overharvesting are devastating vast webs of ocean life, . . . [and] the underwater realm is in peril."

Overfishing Threatens the World's Oceans

Ben Carmichael

Overfishing threatens the marine biodiversity needed to keep the world's oceans healthy, argues Ben Carmichael in the following viewpoint. Studies show that by midcentury so many fish and shellfish species will be depleted that many commercial fisheries will collapse, he maintains. Indeed, Carmichael claims, without biodiversity the world's oceans face difficulties recovering from pollution and destructive bottom trawling. Policies such as marine reserves and fishing quotas will increase biodiversity and the health of the oceans on which humanity depends, he concludes. Carmichael is a regular contributor to OnEarth, *published by the Natural Resources Defense Council.*

As you read, consider the following questions:

1. What species, in addition to those we eat, suffer from overfishing, in Carmichael's opinion?

Ben Carmichael, "Charting a New Course to Save Our Seas: A Landmark Study Offers an Urgent Directive to Revive the Oceans," *OnEarth*, Spring 2007. Copyright © 2007 by the Natural Resources Defense Council. Reproduced by permission.

2. What promising news does the study published in *Science* offer, in the author's view?

3. According to the author, what has California done to increase biodiversity in state waters?

Fish populations are in free fall; the food supply of millions of people around the world is in jeopardy. Seabed-scouring trawlers and reckless overharvesting are devastating vast webs of ocean life, and the species we eat aren't the only ones to suffer. From majestic sea turtles to wondrous deepwater organisms with their startlingly unique arrays of DNA, the underwater realm is in peril.

The Importance of Marine Biodiversity

In reaction to the rapid loss of marine biodiversity, an international team of scientists and economists led by the biologist Boris Worm at Dalhousie University in Halifax, Nova Scotia, published a study in the November 3, 2006, issue of the journal *Science* in which they analyzed more than 50 years' worth of fisheries and ecological monitoring data. All told, the study examined 83 percent of the world catch during that time period to create a comprehensive picture of what the decline in marine biodiversity means for humans. By midcentury, the team concluded, many fish and shellfish species could collapse, their commercial catches reduced to a mere tenth of their historical highs. But the study also offered some promising news: It's not too late. The trend is reversible; ecosystems with the greatest biodiversity appear more able to heal themselves than those with fewer distinct species. With smarter, more forward-looking management, ocean life could rebound.

"This study helps answer one of the central questions in the field of ecology, which is: 'What is the role of biodiversity?'" says Lisa Suatoni, an evolutionary biologist and NRDC [Natural Resources Defense Council] science fellow. "The answer, it seems, is that biodiversity translates into resilience."

Like a healthy immune system, diversity gives oceans the strength to recover from injury, whether caused by overfishing, pollution, or destruction of habitat by trawling. Enabling the seas to heal in this way requires adopting the very principles that NRDC's oceans program works to promote: Create protected marine areas similar to wildlife preserves on land, stop overfishing, and make management decisions that take into account all of the interconnected species within an ecosystem. Species near the top of the food chain—the ones we eat, such as cod and swordfish—could then flourish.

Charting a New Course

It is not only scientists who are realizing the wisdom of such an approach. [In the fall of 2006] California proposed protections for a network of 29 marine areas covering more than 200 square miles of state waters, four times the area of San Francisco. The goal is to create safe havens where a wide range of marine life can coexist unfettered by human activity, thereby boosting biodiversity and replenishing depleted populations. NRDC scientists and policy experts played an instrumental role in gathering support for the state's Marine Life Protection Act, passed in 1999, which paved the way for the new designations; they are now helping to implement the law.

Other states are moving to rehabilitate their waters as well. New York, for example, has passed a law that will encourage the application of more enlightened, interdisciplinary management practices to protect marine species and habitats, from wetland nurseries to deepwater environments. NRDC worked with state agencies and legislators to pass the law and will continue to work with agency officials to promote its implementation.

On a national level, the recent reauthorization of the landmark Magnuson-Stevens Fishery Conservation and Management Act should prove a boon to oceans beyond coastal states' offshore boundaries. The law is named for Senator Ted Stevens, Republican of Alaska, who has proven a consistent supporter of the common-sense idea that the surest way to maintain profitable commercial fisheries, in his home state and elsewhere, is to prevent overfishing. The reauthorization bill, signed into law on January 12, [2007,] strengthens the existing law, passed in 1976, by setting a firm deadline for ending overfishing and requiring the use of current scientific data in establishing quotas. Working closely with key Senate and House staff members, NRDC brought its legal, scientific, and economic expertise to the debate and played a leading role in the reauthorization process.

"This is about protecting some of our most magnificent places and safeguarding the well-being of millions of people who rely on them," says Karen Garrison, an NRDC oceans policy expert. "The underwater world is as precious, as wild and beautiful—and as necessary—as the wilderness of Yosemite. But we are playing catch-up in the oceans."

| "This [fisheries collapse] prediction has zero credibility within the scientific community."

The Threat Posed by Overfishing Is Exaggerated

Jim Hutchinson Jr.

Studies claiming that the world's fisheries are in imminent danger of collapse are based on flawed methodologies, asserts Jim Hutchinson Jr. in the following viewpoint. For example, he contends, fish stock statistics based on catch rates rather than actual stock analysis are inaccurate. Lower catch rates are the result of tight regulations, not actual stock reduction, Hutchinson argues. Studies funded by prominent environmental groups are biased and designed not to develop fair and flexible fishing policies, but to close down fishing businesses. Hutchinson is executive editor of the Fisherman Magazine.

As you read, consider the following questions:

1. According to fisheries scientist Ray Hilborn, as cited by the author, what is the true status of the Georges Bank haddock stock?

Jim Hutchinson Jr., "Falling for Fisheries Collapse Hook, Line, Sinker," *SeaCoast Online*, December 16, 2007. Reproduced by permission.

2. In Hutchinson's opinion, who actually provides the doomsday predictions and headlines about U.S. fisheries that appear in the media?

3. When does the Pew Environmental Group campaign against fishing begin each year, according to the author?

The journal *Science* released a report [in December 2006] by scientist Boris Worm that predicted a total collapse of our global fisheries. The press releases in support of the study were generated by Pew Charitable Trusts—the group responsible for funding the study—and the headlines were so dramatic that newspapers across the country had no choice but to run them front and center: "Fisheries Collapse Imminent" or "World's Fish to Disappear by 2048."

Challenging the Predictions

When the dust from the doom and gloom settled, a collective of non-Pew funded scientists came out against the report, but without the estimated annual operating revenue of around $70 million, which is what the Pew Environment Group boasts; few newspapers ever heard the criticisms.

"This particular prediction has zero credibility within the scientific community," said Ray Hilborn, fisheries scientist at the University of Washington in Seattle following the release of the Worm findings, which he claimed "cannot be taken seriously."

One of Hilborn's key contentions was that the scientists involved in the research had utilized faulty methodologies, most notably in the use of catch rates as opposed to stock analysis.

"One of the stocks they list as collapsed is the Georges Bank haddock stock, which is bigger now than it has been in 40 years. The catch is lower simply because the regulations are much tighter," Hilborn said.

Worm himself even followed up on the criticism by blaming the "media" for taking his words out of context.

The Consequences of Agenda-Driven Science

Agenda-driven science, particularly when it's confused with or substituted for real (meaning objective) science, is a threat to all of us. This won't come as a revelation to anyone associated with commercial fishing; professional fear merchants have been making doom and gloom predictions about the future of our fisheries for years. We've been suffering the consequences.

Nils Stolpe,
National Fisherman, *March 2006.*

"They (the media) treat this as a prediction, as if we said that it will collapse by 2050, which is different from what we actually said—which is, if the present trend that we're seeing worldwide continues, we would see widespread collapse of fisheries by 2050," Worm told *CBC News.*

Falling for Old Tricks

Of course, it wasn't really the "media" that gave the doomsday predictions and headlines, it was Pew itself. The Pew Environment Group is up to its annual tricks, and newspapers like the *Portsmouth [NH] Herald* are falling for it again, hook, line and sinker.

"Not only does chronic overfishing harm fish populations and reduce commercial and recreational fishing opportunities," said Gerry Leape, president of the Marine Fish Conservation Network [MFCN], "but by one estimate, Americans have lost three billion dollars annually in exports, jobs, recreation and other economic activity."

Leape is not only the president of MFCN, he's also in charge of marine conservation with the National Environmental Trust [NET], which recently merged operations with Pew Charitable Trusts.

With 23 years of political fundraising and advocacy experience, including a 10-year stint with Greenpeace, Leape is regarded as one of the top lobbyists in the environmental business community.

Pew is actively fighting against leaders of both the commercial and recreational fishing community along the East Coast who are seeking fairness and flexibility in fisheries management so they can stay in business; Leape and his Pew Environment Group are unwilling to acknowledge that rebuilding targets and time frames are arbitrary and inflexible, and would rather put people out of business while forcing Americans to stop fishing for species like summer flounder, scup, sea bass and tautog.

Manipulating Facts

Those folks who are in the business of fishing along the East Coast will tell you that the data being used by those in the environmental business community is faulty, manipulated and financed by groups who want to shut down their businesses.

On the other hand, environmental business leaders like Leape have a $70 million Pew war chest at their disposal, so no matter whether the data's good or bad, it's easy to get it into the right hands when you can afford the best PR [public relations].

A perfect example is Leape's use of an estimate that $3 billion has been lost due to reduced fishing activities. The "estimate" in question comes from a single page of a 1996 forecasting report from the National Oceanic and Atmospheric Administration called "NOAA Strategic Plan: A Vision for 2005." That's according to Leape's co-worker at NET, Tara Losoff.

In addition to long-range forecasting, the four-page report in question that Leape and his lobbyists are relying on as "best available science" also relies on global fisheries data from 1989.

Things have changed in those 20 years of fisheries and forecasting. As Pew Environment Group continues to grow stronger and spread more of its money around on anti-fishing research and rhetoric, mainstream news organizations like the *Portsmouth Herald* may continue to get duped into running unedited versions of this hyperbole and outlandishness. That is, until news editors start to recognize these press releases for what they really are—political action statements and public relation campaigns propagated by the radical environmental business community.

Not coincidentally, this campaign hits its stride every year at this time, as this is when fisheries management representatives get together to set annual catch limits for the following year.

It's also when these same environmental business leaders are attempting to hammer their message home to the cherry [new] senators and congressmen they helped get elected earlier in November.

The environment is for sale, and I think most editors and readers alike would be surprised to learn who's doing the buying.

"*Industrial society is overdosing the oceans with basic nutrients— the . . . compounds that curl out of smokestacks and tailpipes [and] wash into the sea from fertilized lawns and cropland.*"

Runoff Pollution Threatens the World's Oceans

Kenneth R. Weiss

The runoff from modern life is polluting the world's oceans with excess nutrients and toxic chemicals, claims Kenneth R. Weiss in the following viewpoint. Pollutants absorbed by the ocean from fertilized lawns and crops, from streets and sewers, and from industry and automobiles feed the growth of toxic algae and bacteria, he maintains. Moreover, Weiss argues, overfishing has depleted the ocean life that normally checks these toxic life forms. Environmental pressures have so altered the world's oceans that they no longer have the resiliency to recover, he contends. Weiss is a staff writer for the Los Angeles Times.

As you read, consider the following questions:

1. According to Weiss, what is one of many symptoms of a "virulent pox" on the world's oceans?

2. What changed Jeremy Jackson's belief in the sea's inexhaustible capacity to heal itself, according to the author?

3. How does Weiss explain the process of "fishing down the food web"?

[In] Moreton Bay, Australia, the fireweed began each spring as tufts of hairy growth and spread across the seafloor fast enough to cover a football field in an hour.

A Venomous Weed

When fishermen touched it, their skin broke out in searing welts. Their lips blistered and peeled. Their eyes burned and swelled shut. Water that splashed from their nets spread the inflammation to their legs and torsos.

"It comes up like little boils," said Randolph Van Dyk, a fisherman whose powerful legs are pocked with scars. "At nighttime, you can feel them burning. I tried everything to get rid of them. Nothing worked."

As the weed blanketed miles of the bay over the last decade, it stained fishing nets a dark purple and left them coated with a powdery residue. When fishermen tried to shake it off the webbing, their throats constricted and they gasped for air.

After one man bit a fishing line in two, his mouth and tongue swelled so badly that he couldn't eat solid food for a week. Others made an even more painful mistake, neglecting to wash the residue from their hands before relieving themselves over the sides of their boats.

For a time, embarrassment kept them from talking publicly about their condition. When they finally did speak up, authorities dismissed their complaints—until a bucket of the hairy weed made it to the University of Queensland's marine botany lab.

Samples placed in a drying oven gave off fumes so strong that professors and students ran out of the building and into the street, choking and coughing.

Scientist Judith O'Neil put a tiny sample under a microscope and peered at the long black filaments. Consulting a botanical reference, she identified the weed as a strain of cyanobacteria, an ancestor of modern-day bacteria and algae that flourished 2.7 billion years ago.

O'Neil, a biological oceanographer, was familiar with these ancient life forms, but had never seen this particular kind before. What was it doing in Moreton Bay? Why was it so toxic? Why was it growing so fast?

The venomous weed, known to scientists as *Lyngbya majuscula*, has appeared in at least a dozen other places around the globe. It is one of many symptoms of a virulent pox on the world's oceans.

In many places—the atolls of the Pacific, the shrimp beds of the Eastern Seaboard, the fiords of Norway—some of the most advanced forms of ocean life are struggling to survive while the most primitive are thriving and spreading. Fish, corals and marine mammals are dying while algae, bacteria and jellyfish are growing unchecked. Where this pattern is most pronounced, scientists evoke a scenario of evolution running in reverse, returning to the primeval seas of hundreds of millions of years ago.

The Rise of Slime

Jeremy B.C. Jackson, a marine ecologist and paleontologist at the Scripps Institution of Oceanography in La Jolla [California], says we are witnessing "the rise of slime."

For many years, it was assumed that the oceans were too vast for humanity to damage in any lasting way. "Man marks the Earth with ruin," wrote the 19th century poet Lord Byron. "His control stops with the shore."

Even in modern times, when oil spills, chemical discharges and other industrial accidents heightened awareness of man's capacity to injure sea life, the damage was often regarded as temporary.

But over time, the accumulation of environmental pressures has altered the basic chemistry of the seas.

The causes are varied, but collectively they have made the ocean more hospitable to primitive organisms by putting too much food into the water.

Industrial society is overdosing the oceans with basic nutrients—the nitrogen, carbon, iron and phosphorous compounds that curl out of smokestacks and tailpipes, wash into the sea from fertilized lawns and cropland, seep out of septic tanks and gush from sewer pipes.

Modern industry and agriculture produce more fixed nitrogen—fertilizer, essentially—than all natural processes on land. Millions of tons of carbon dioxide and nitrogen oxide, produced by burning fossil fuels, enter the ocean every day.

These pollutants feed excessive growth of harmful algae and bacteria.

At the same time, overfishing and destruction of wetlands have diminished the competing sea life and natural buffers that once held the microbes and weeds in check.

The consequences are evident worldwide.

Off the coast of Sweden each summer, blooms of cyanobacteria turn the Baltic Sea into a stinking, yellow-brown slush that locals call "rhubarb soup." Dead fish bob in the surf. If people get too close, their eyes burn and they have trouble breathing.

On the southern coast of Maui in the Hawaiian Islands, high tide leaves piles of green-brown algae that smell so foul condominium owners have hired a tractor driver to scrape them off the beach every morning.

On Florida's Gulf Coast, residents complain that harmful algae blooms have become bigger, more frequent and longer-lasting. Toxins from these red tides have killed hundreds of sea mammals and caused emergency rooms to fill up with coastal residents suffering respiratory distress.

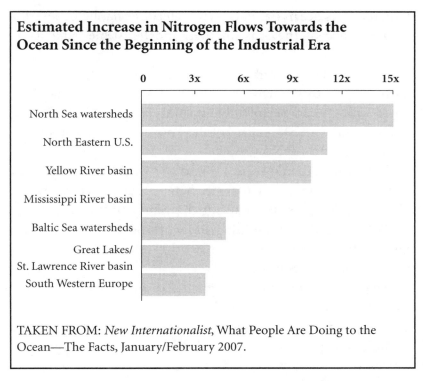

Estimated Increase in Nitrogen Flows Towards the Ocean Since the Beginning of the Industrial Era

TAKEN FROM: *New Internationalist*, What People Are Doing to the Ocean—The Facts, January/February 2007.

North of Venice, Italy, a sticky mixture of algae and bacteria collects on the Adriatic Sea in spring and summer. This white mucus washes ashore, fouling beaches, or congeals into submerged blobs, some bigger than a person.

Along the Spanish coast, jellyfish swarm so thick that nets are strung to protect swimmers from their sting.

Organisms such as the fireweed that torments the fishermen of Moreton Bay have been around for eons. They emerged from the primordial ooze and came to dominate ancient oceans that were mostly lifeless. Over time, higher forms of life gained supremacy. Now they are under siege.

Losing the Capacity to Heal

Like other scientists, Jeremy Jackson, 63, was slow to perceive this latest shift in the biological order. He has spent a good part of his professional life underwater. Though he had seen firsthand that ocean habitats were deteriorating, he believed in the resilience of the seas, in their inexhaustible capacity to heal themselves.

Then came the hurricane season of 1980. A Category 5 storm ripped through waters off the north coast of Jamaica, where Jackson had been studying corals since the late 1960s. A majestic stand of staghorn corals, known as "the Haystacks," was turned into rubble.

Scientists gathered from around the world to examine the damage. They wrote a paper predicting that the corals would rebound quickly, as they had for thousands of years.

"We were the best ecologists, working on what was the best-studied coral reef in the world, and we got it 100% wrong," Jackson recalled.

The vividly colored reef, which had nurtured a wealth of fish species, never recovered.

"Why did I get it wrong?" Jackson asked. He now sees that the quiet creep of environmental decay, occurring largely unnoticed over many years, had drastically altered the ocean.

As tourist resorts sprouted along the Jamaican coast, sewage, fertilizer and other nutrients washed into the sea. Overfishing removed most of the grazing fish that kept algae under control. Warmer waters encouraged bacterial growth and further stressed the corals.

For a time, these changes were masked by algae-eating sea urchins. But when disease greatly reduced their numbers, the reef was left defenseless. The corals were soon smothered by a carpet of algae and bacteria. Today, the reef is largely a boneyard of coral skeletons.

Many of the same forces have wiped out 80% of the corals in the Caribbean, despoiled two-thirds of the estuaries in the United States and destroyed 75% of California's kelp forests, once prime habitat for fish.

Jackson uses a homespun analogy to illustrate what is happening. The world's 6 billion inhabitants, he says, have failed to follow a homeowner's rule of thumb: Be careful what you dump in the swimming pool, and make sure the filter is working.

"We're pushing the oceans back to the dawn of evolution," Jackson said, "a half-billion years ago when the oceans were ruled by jellyfish and bacteria."

Growing Jellyfish Population

The 55-foot commercial trawler working the Georgia coast sagged under the burden of a hefty catch. The cables pinged and groaned as if about to snap.

Working the power winch, ropes and pulleys, Grovea Simpson hoisted the net and its dripping catch over the rear deck. With a tug on the trip-rope, the bulging sack unleashed its massive load.

Plop. Splat. Whoosh. About 2,000 pounds of cannonball jellyfish slopped onto the deck. The jiggling, cantaloupe-size blobs ricocheted around the stern and slid down an opening into the boat's ice-filled hold.

The deck was streaked with purple-brown contrails of slimy residue; a stinging, ammonia-like odor filled the air.

"That's the smell of money," Simpson said, all smiles at the haul. "Jellyballs are thick today. Seven cents a pound. Yes, sir, we're making money."

Simpson would never eat a jellyfish. But shrimp have grown scarce in these waters after decades of intensive trawling. So during the winter months when jellyfish swarm, he makes his living catching what he used to consider a messy nuisance clogging his nets.

It's simple math. He can spend a week at sea scraping the ocean bottom for shrimp and be lucky to pocket $600 after paying for fuel, food, wages for crew and the boat owner's cut.

Or, in a few hours of trawling for jellyfish, he can fill up the hold, be back in port the same day and clear twice as much. The jellyfish are processed at the dock in Darien, Ga., and exported to China and Japan, where spicy jellyfish salad and soup are delicacies.

"Easy money," Simpson said. "They get so thick you can walk on them."

Jellyfish populations are growing because they can. The fish that used to compete with them for food have become scarce because of overfishing. The sea turtles that once preyed on them are nearly gone. And the plankton they love to eat are growing explosively.

As their traditional catch declines, fishermen around the world now haul in 450,000 tons of jellyfish per year, more than twice as much as a decade ago.

Fishing Down the Food Web

This is a logical step in a process that Daniel Pauly, a fisheries scientist at the University of British Columbia, calls "fishing down the food web." Fishermen first went after the largest and most popular fish, such as tuna, swordfish, cod and grouper. When those stocks were depleted, they pursued other prey, often smaller and lower on the food chain.

"We are eating bait and moving on to jellyfish and plankton," Pauly said.

In California waters, for instance, three of the top five commercial catches are not even fish. They are squid, crabs and sea urchins.

This is what remains of California's historic fishing industry, once known for the sardine fishery attached to Monterey's Cannery Row and the world's largest tuna fleet, based in San Diego, which brought American kitchens StarKist, Bumble Bee and Chicken of the Sea.

Overfishing began centuries ago but accelerated dramatically after World War II, when new technologies armed industrial fleets with sonar, satellite data and global positioning systems, allowing them to track schools of fish and find their most remote habitats.

The result is that the population of big fish has declined by 90% over the last 50 years.

It's reached the point that the world's fishermen, though more numerous, working harder and sailing farther than ever, are catching fewer fish. The global catch has been declining since the late 1980s, an analysis by Pauly and colleague Reg Watson showed.

The reduction isn't readily apparent in the fish markets of wealthy countries, where people are willing to pay high prices for exotic fare from distant oceans—slimeheads caught off New Zealand and marketed as orange roughy, or Patagonian toothfish, renamed Chilean sea bass. Now, both of those fish are becoming scarce.

Fish farming also exacts a toll. To feed the farmed stocks, menhaden, sardines and anchovies are harvested in great quantities, ground up and processed into pellets.

Dense schools of these small fish once swam the world's estuaries and coastal waters, inhaling plankton like swarming clouds of silvery vacuum cleaners. Maryland's Chesapeake Bay, the nation's largest estuary, used to be clear, its waters filtered every three days by piles of oysters so numerous that their reefs posed a hazard to navigation. All this has changed.

A Microbial Soup

There and in many other places, bacteria and algae run wild in the absence of the many mouths that once ate them. As the depletion of fish allows the lowest forms of life to run rampant, said Pauly, it is "transforming the oceans into a microbial soup."

Jellyfish are flourishing in the soup, demonstrating their ability to adapt to wholesale changes—including the growing human appetite for them. Jellyfish have been around, after all, at least 500 million years, longer than most marine animals.

In the Black Sea, an Atlantic comb jelly carried in the ballast water of a ship from the East Coast of the United States took over waters saturated with farm runoff. Free of predators, the jellies gorged on plankton and fish larvae, depleting the fisheries on which the Russian and Turkish fleets depend. The plague subsided only with the accidental importation of another predatory jellyfish that ate the comb jellies.

Federal scientists tallied a tenfold increase in jellies in the Bering Sea in the 1990s. They were so thick off the Alaskan Peninsula that fishermen nicknamed it the Slime Bank. Researchers have found teeming swarms of jellyfish off Georges Bank in New England and the coast of Namibia, in the fiords of Norway and in the Gulf of Mexico. Also proliferating is the giant nomurai found off Japan, a jellyfish the size of a washing machine.

Most jellies are smaller than a fist, but their sheer numbers have gummed up fishing nets, forced the shutdown of power plants by clogging intake pipes, stranded cruise liners and disrupted operations of the world's largest aircraft carrier, the *Ronald Reagan*.

Of the 2,000 or so identified jellyfish species, only about 10 are commercially harvested. The largest fisheries are off China and other Asian nations. New ones are springing up in Australia, the United States, England, Namibia, Turkey and Canada as fishermen look for ways to stay in business.

Pauly, 60, predicts that future generations will see nothing odd or unappetizing about a plateful of these gelatinous blobs.

"My kids," Pauly said, "will tell their children: Eat your jellyfish."

"At the current rate of increase, ocean acidity ... would devastate many species of fish and other animals that have thrived in chemically stable seawater for millions of years."

Acidification Threatens the World's Oceans

Usha Lee McFarling

Since the Industrial Revolution began, the oceans have been absorbing increasing amounts of carbon dioxide (CO_2) from the air, observes Usha Lee McFarling in the following viewpoint. As a result, she claims, the world's oceans have become increasingly more acidic. While algae and bacteria can survive in acidic seas, many marine species cannot, McFarling maintains. Indeed, she asserts, acidic seas deplete the chemicals that shellfish and corals need to make their shells and skeletons. If the amount of CO_2 continues to increase, McFarling argues, the oceans, nature's CO_2 pump, will no longer be able to stem the impact of global warming. McFarling is a staff writer for the Los Angeles Times.

As you read, consider the following questions:

1. In McFarling's view, at the current rate of increase, how much more acidic will the oceans be at the end of this century than they were before the Industrial Revolution?

2. How many tons of carbon dioxide do scientists estimate have been absorbed by the oceans since the start of the Industrial Revolution, according to the author?

3. What forms of life are likely to be the first victims of ocean acidification, in McFarling's opinion?

As she stared down into a wide-mouthed plastic jar aboard the R/V [research vessel] *Discoverer*, Victoria Fabry peered into the future.

The marine snails she was studying—graceful creatures with winglike feet that help them glide through the water—had started to dissolve.

Fabry was taken aback. The button-sized snails, called pteropods, are hardy animals that swirl in dense patches in some of the world's coldest seas. In 20 years of studying the snails, a vital ingredient in the polar food supply, the marine biologist from Cal State San Marcos had never seen such damage.

In a brief experiment aboard the federal research vessel plowing through rough Alaskan seas, the pteropods were sealed in jars. The carbon dioxide they exhaled made the water inside more acidic. Though slight, this change in water chemistry ravaged the snails' translucent shells. After 36 hours, they were pitted and covered with white spots.

An Invisible Change

The one-liter jars of seawater were a microcosm of change now occurring invisibly throughout the world's vast, open seas.

As industrial activity pumps massive amounts of carbon dioxide into the environment, more of the gas is being absorbed by the oceans. As a result, seawater is becoming more acidic, and a variety of sea creatures await the same dismal fate as Fabry's pteropods.

The greenhouse gas, best known for accumulating in the atmosphere and heating the planet, is entering the ocean at a rate of nearly 1 million tons per hour—10 times the natural rate.

Scientists report that the seas are more acidic today than they have been in at least 650,000 years. At the current rate of increase, ocean acidity is expected, by the end of this century, to be 2 1/2 times what it was before the Industrial Revolution began 200 years ago. Such a change would devastate many species of fish and other animals that have thrived in chemically stable seawater for millions of years.

Less likely to be harmed are algae, bacteria and other primitive forms of life that are already proliferating at the expense of fish, marine mammals and corals.

In a matter of decades, the world's remaining coral reefs could be too brittle to withstand pounding waves. Shells could become too fragile to protect their occupants. By the end of the century, much of the polar ocean is expected to be as acidified as the water that did such damage to the pteropods aboard the *Discoverer*.

Some marine biologists predict that altered acid levels will disrupt fisheries by melting away the bottom rungs of the food chain—tiny planktonic plants and animals that provide the basic nutrition for all living things in the sea.

Fabry, who recently testified on the issue before the U.S. Senate, told policymakers that the effects on marine life could be "direct and profound."

"The potential is there to have a devastating impact," Fabry said, "for the oceans to be very, very different in the near future than they are today."

Abusing the Global Safety Valve

The oceans have been a natural sponge for carbon dioxide from time immemorial. Especially after calamities such as asteroid strikes, they have acted as a global safety valve, soaking up excess CO_2 and preventing catastrophic overheating of the planet.

If not for the oceans, the Earth would have warmed by 2 degrees instead of 1 over the last century, scientists say. Glaciers would be disappearing faster than they are, droughts would be more widespread and rising sea levels would be more pronounced.

When carbon dioxide is added to the ocean gradually, it does little harm. Some of it is taken up during photosynthesis by microscopic plants called phytoplankton. Some of it is used by microorganisms to build shells. After their inhabitants die, the empty shells rain down on the seafloor in a kind of biological snow. The famed white cliffs of Dover are made of this material.

Today, however, the addition of carbon dioxide to the seas is anything but gradual.

Scientists estimate that nearly 500 billion tons of the gas have been absorbed by the oceans since the start of the Industrial Revolution. That is more than a fourth of all the CO_2 that humanity has emitted into the atmosphere. Eventually, 80% of all human-generated carbon dioxide is expected to find its way into the sea.

Carbon dioxide moves freely between air and sea in a process known as molecular diffusion. The exchange occurs in a film of water at the surface. Carbon dioxide travels wherever concentrations are lowest. If levels in the atmosphere are high, the gas goes into the ocean. If they are higher in the sea, as they have been for much of the past, the gas leaves the water and enters the air.

If not for the CO_2 pumped into the skies in the last century, more of the gas would leave the sea than would enter it.

Sopping Up CO_2

The atmosphere has 30% more CO_2 than it did 200 years ago. As the level of CO_2 has risen, so has the amount the oceans have absorbed. In fact, if it weren't for the oceans' ability to sop up CO_2, say scientists, global warming would actually be twice as intense as it is today.

That's the good news. Now the bad: That extra CO_2 has altered the oceans' acidity.

Hugh Westrup, Current Science, *November 3, 2006.*

"We have reversed that direction," said Ken Caldeira, an expert on ocean chemistry and carbon dioxide at the Carnegie Institution's department of global ecology, based at Stanford University.

Destructive Carbonic Acid

When carbon dioxide mixes with seawater, it creates carbonic acid, the weak acid in carbonated drinks.

Increased acidity reduces the abundance of the right chemical forms of a mineral called calcium carbonate, which corals and other sea animals need to build shells and skeletons. It also slows the growth of the animals within those shells.

Even slightly acidified seawater is toxic to the eggs and larvae of some fish species. In others, including amberjack and halibut, it can cause heart attacks, experiments show. Acidified waters also tend to asphyxiate animals that require a lot of oxygen, such as fast-swimming squid.

The pH scale, a measure of how acidic or alkaline a substance is, ranges from 1 to 14, with 7 being neutral. The lower the pH, the greater the acidity. Each number represents a ten-fold change in acidity or alkalinity.

For more than a decade, teams led by Richard Feely, a chemical oceanographer at the National Oceanic and Atmospheric Administration's Pacific Marine Environmental Laboratory in Seattle, have traveled from Antarctica to the Aleutian Islands, taking tens of thousands of water samples to gauge how the ocean's acidity is changing.

By comparing these measurements to past levels of carbon dioxide preserved in ice cores, the researchers determined that the average pH of the ocean surface has declined since the beginning of the Industrial Revolution by 0.1 units, from 8.16 to 8.05.

Geological records show that such a change has not occurred in 650,000 years, Feely said.

In April [2006], Feely returned from a cruise to the North Pacific, where he took pH measurements at locations the team first sampled in 1991. This time, Feely's group found that the average pH in surface waters had dropped an additional 0.025 units in 15 years—a relatively large change for such a short time.

The measurements confirm those taken in the 1990s and indicate that forecasts of increased acidity are on target, Feely said.

If CO_2 emissions continue at their current pace, the pH of the ocean is expected to dip to 7.9 or lower by the end of the century—a 150% change.

The last time ocean chemistry underwent such a radical transformation, Caldeira said, "was when the dinosaurs went extinct."

Until recently, the ocean was seen as a potential reservoir for greenhouse gases. Scientists explored the possibility that carbon dioxide could be trapped in smokestacks, compressed into a gooey liquid and piped directly into the deep sea.

The Impact on Sea Life

Then the results of Jim Barry's experiments started trickling in.

A biologist at the Monterey Bay Aquarium Research Institute, Barry wanted to know what would happen to sea creatures in the vicinity of a large dose of carbon dioxide.

He anchored a set of small plastic rings onto the seafloor to create an enclosure and sent a robot down to squirt liquid carbon dioxide into the surrounding water. Then he waited to see what would happen to animals in the enclosures and those that happened to swim through the CO_2 cloud.

Sea stars, sea cucumbers and sea urchins died immediately. Eighty percent of animals within three feet of the carbon dioxide died. Animals 15 feet away also perished in large numbers.

"When they were adjacent to the CO_2 plume, pretty much, it killed everything," Barry said.

Experiments in Germany, Norway and Japan produced similar results. The evidence persuaded the U.S. Department of Energy, which had spent $22 million on such research, including Barry's, to pull the plug. Instead, the department will study the possibility of storing carbon dioxide in the ground and on decreasing emissions at their source.

Scientists say the acidification of the oceans won't be arrested unless the output of CO_2 from factories, power plants and automobiles is substantially reduced. Even now, the problem may be irreversible.

"One thing we know for certain is it's not going to be a good thing for the ocean," Barry said. "We just don't know how bad it will be."

Scientists predict the effect will be felt first in the polar oceans and at lower depths, because cold water absorbs more carbon dioxide than warm water. One area of immediate concern is the Bering Sea and other waters around Alaska, home to half of the commercial U.S. fish and shellfish catch.

Because of acidification, waters in the Bering Sea about 280 feet down are running short of the materials that corals and other animals need to grow shells and skeletons. These chemical building blocks are normally abundant at such depths. In coming decades, the impoverished zone is expected to reach closer to the surface. A great quantity of sea life would then be affected.

"I'm getting nervous about that," Feely said.

The First Victims

The first victims of acidification are likely to be cold-water corals that provide food, shelter and reproductive grounds for hundreds of species, including commercially valuable ones such as sea bass, snapper, ocean perch and rock shrimp.

By the end of the century, 70% of cold-water corals will be exposed to waters stripped of the chemicals required for sturdy skeletons, said John Guinotte, an expert on corals at the nonprofit Marine Conservation Biology Institute in Bellevue, Wash.

"I liken it to osteoporosis in humans," Guinotte said. "You just can't build a strong structure without the right materials."

Cold-water corals, which thrive in waters as deep as three miles, were discovered only two decades ago. They harbor sponges, which show promise as powerful anti-cancer and antiviral agents; the AIDS drug AZT was formulated using clues from a coral sponge. Scientists fear that these unique ecosystems may be obliterated before they can be fully utilized or appreciated.

Tropical corals will not be affected as quickly because they live in warmer waters that do not absorb as much carbon dioxide. But in 100 years, large tropical reefs—called rain forests of the sea because of their biodiversity—may survive only in patches near the equator.

"Twenty-five percent of all species in the ocean live part of their life cycle on coral reefs. We're afraid we're going to lose these habitats and these species," said Chris Langdon, a coral expert at the University of Miami who has conducted experiments showing that corals grow more slowly when exposed to acidified waters.

Warm-water corals are already dying at high rates as global warming heats oceans and causes corals to "bleach"—lose or expel the symbiotic algae that provide vivid color and nutrients necessary for survival. Pollution, trampling by tourists and dynamiting by fishermen also take a devastating toll. An estimated 20% of the world's corals have disappeared since 1980.

"Corals are getting squeezed from both ends," said Joanie Kleypas, a marine ecologist and coral expert at the National Center for Atmospheric Research in Boulder, Colo.

The question for scientists is whether living things will adapt to acidification. Will some animals migrate to warmer waters that don't lose shell-building minerals as quickly? Will some survive despite the new chemistry? Will complex marine food chains be harmed?

One laboratory experiment showed that a strain of shelled plankton thrived in higher CO_2 conditions. But most research has shown that shelled animals and corals stop growing or are damaged.

"We put a lot of faith in the idea that organisms can adapt," Kleypas said, "but organisms have probably not evolved to handle these big changes."

A Global Warming Event

The best analogy to what is occurring today is in the fossil records of a 55-million-year-old event known as the Paleocene-Eocene Thermal Maximum, when the Earth underwent one of the most abrupt and extreme global warming events in history.

The average temperature of the planet rose 9 degrees because of an increase in greenhouse gases. Balmy 70-degree days were common in the Arctic. The sudden warming shifted entire ecosystems to higher and cooler latitudes and drove myriad ocean species to extinction.

Geologists agree that a great warming occurred as a result of greenhouse gases, but until recently were uncertain about the volume of gas involved or how much the acidity of the oceans changed.

James Zachos, a paleo-oceanographer at [the University of California at] Santa Cruz, made an important discovery in 2003 by drilling into seabed sediments more than two miles beneath the ocean's surface. This muck contains layers of microscopic plankton shells. Their chemical composition reveals what ocean conditions were like when they formed.

Zachos' international team analyzed sediments from a series of cores taken from the floor of the Atlantic Ocean 750 miles west of Namibia. At the bottom of the cores, the team found normal sediments, rich in calcium carbonate from shells—the sign of a healthy ocean.

But higher up, at a point in geologic history when the last major global warming event occurred, the whitish, carbonate-rich ooze gave way to a dark red clay layer free of shells. That condition, the researchers concluded, was caused by a highly acidified ocean. This state of affairs lasted for 40,000 or 50,000 years. It took 60,000 years before the ocean recovered and the sediments appeared normal again.

In a paper published [in 2005] in the journal *Science*, Zachos' team concluded that only a massive release of carbon dioxide could have caused both extreme warming and acidification of ocean waters.

Zachos estimated that 4.5 trillion tons of carbon entered the atmosphere to trigger the event.

It could take modern civilization just 300 years to unleash the same quantity of carbon, according to a variety of projections by researchers.

"This will be a much greater shock," Zachos said. "The change in modern surface ocean pH will be much more extreme than it was 55 million years ago."

Periodical Bibliography

The following articles have been selected to supplement the diverse views presented in this chapter.

Tundi Agardi	"The Alarming pH Factor," *Fish Information & Services*, April 21, 2007.
Joel K. Bourne	"Loving Our Coasts to Death," *National Geographic*, July 2006.
Mark Hertsgaard	"Mutiny for the Bounty," *Nation*, January 29, 2007.
Rowan Hooper	"Sea Life in Peril as Oceans Turn Acid," *New Scientist*, July 9–15, 2006.
Gerald Leape	"Standing Up for Fisheries, Fishing Communities," *SeaCoast Online*, February 3, 2008. www.seacoastonline.com.
Andrew Myers	"What Comes Around: Breaking the Cycle of Plastics in the Ocean," *Ocean Conservancy*, Autumn 2007.
David Ransom	"Planet Ocean," *New Internationalist*, January/February 2007.
Dick Russell and Jessie Benton	"The Eye of a Marlin," *Patagonia*, Spring 2006.
Nils Stolpe	"An Homage to Michael Crichton," *National Fisherman*, March 2006.
Kenneth R. Weiss	"The Rise of Slime: The Run-Off from Modern Life Is Feeding an Explosion of Primitive Organisms," *New Internationalist*, January/February 2007.
Jonathan Yardley	"The End of Infinity/The End of Bounty/The Exhaustible Sea; How Humans Imperil the Oceans and All That Lives in Them," *Washington Post*, July 29, 2007.

CHAPTER 2

What Ocean Policies Are Best?

Chapter Preface

Following the devastation of Hurricane Katrina, many scientists suggested that had the wetlands and barrier islands that once separated New Orleans from the Gulf of Mexico not been sacrificed to support coastal development, the toll of Katrina would have been significantly reduced. Beaches, barrier islands, and wetlands do indeed serve as barriers to the ferocity of storms; however, to maintain coastal areas for the people that visit and inhabit them, developers have built seawalls and jetties and filled in wetlands and swamps. Not only has this development limited the buffering effect of the natural landscape, it has also destroyed the habitat of many marine species, disrupting the coastal ecology. While few dispute the damaging impact of coastal development, commentators do dispute how best to protect America's coastal marine resources. Some environmentalists claim that governments should strengthen rules that prohibit destructive coastal development. Opponents contend that government interference is counterproductive.

Those hoping to reduce coastal development and the threat it poses to the marine ecology believe that strong laws are necessary to protect these areas. Coastal development permits, they argue, are too easy to obtain. Matt McLain of the Surfrider Foundation, a grassroots environmental organization, for example, would "like to see state agencies be a lot more judicious in how they hand out permits." McLain claims that many state laws concerning coastal development encourage people to look for loopholes that will allow them to build without considering the impact on the coastal environment. For example, a California law that limits new development in beachfront areas exempts owners of homes built before a certain date from the ban on seawalls. Contrary to common wisdom, seawalls actually accelerate erosion because waves hit them much harder than they do natural beaches. According to McLain, people circumvent the law by buying and demolishing older homes to build new homes with beach-destroying seawalls. Consequently, due to the loophole in the law, people can build new homes without considering the environmental consequences.

Free-market environmentalists assert that strict rules and regulations do not work. In fact, these analysts argue, strict laws encourage people to seek out loopholes. R.J. Smith, a scholar at the libertarian Competitive Enterprise Institute, suggests that people are more likely to consider the impact of their behavior if they are rewarded rather than punished. Smith believes that coastal development laws should be modeled after the Department of Agriculture's Conservation Reserve Program, in which some farmers were paid to retire their cropland to wildlife-habitat conservation. Smith claims that while it might appear to be against their best interest, farmers dedicate their land to conservation "because an agent comes to the farmer's door with a check in his hand." A similar program could help conserve coastal communities, Smith concludes. Free-market environmentalists also believe that property owners should be responsible for the risks of owning coastal property. Smith maintains that people should be able to build on a high-risk barrier island if they want to; however, he reasons, these property owners must pay for bridges to the mainland, sewage removal, and flood insurance—costs that governments normally pay. Smith argues that federally subsidized flood insurance only encourages people to build in high-risk areas, plus, they are unfair. "Why should people who deliberately take the very high risks be subsidized by people in safer places?" Smith asks.

Whether coastal marine environments are best protected by carrots or sticks remains to be seen. The authors in the following chapter present their views on what ocean policies they believe are best.

> *"The pristine ocean cruisers we see in TV commercials are also massive ocean polluters, often dumping wastes equivalent to those of a small city into our coastal waters."*

Federal Regulations Are Necessary to Reduce Cruise Ship Pollution

Sam Farr

In the following viewpoint, Sam Farr argues that strict federal regulations are necessary to reduce cruise-ship pollution in U.S. waters. Cruise ships generate as much waste as small cities and dump this waste as close as a little over three miles from U.S. shores, he maintains. Voluntary pollution regulations by cruise lines have proved inadequate to protect America's fragile marine ecosystems, Farr claims. Indeed, he concludes, only strict federal laws that prohibit dumping within twelve miles will prevent cruise ship pollution of U.S. coastal waters. Farr is a Democratic congressman from California.

As you read, consider the following questions:

1. According to Farr, how much sewage does a three-thousand-passenger cruise ship generate?

2. What examples does Farr provide of the failure of voluntary waste-management protocols?

3. How many passengers does the author claim cruise ships carry through America's fragile marine ecosystems each year?

The past 20 years have been good for the cruise industry, and in turn good for the travel industry and the local economies of port towns. But the pristine ocean cruisers we see in TV commercials are also massive ocean polluters, often generating and dumping wastes equivalent to those of a small city into our coastal waters.

In a single week, just one 3,000-passenger cruise ship generates 210,000 gallons of sewage, 1 million gallons of "gray water" (from showers, sinks and dishwater), 37,000 gallons of oily bilge water, millions of gallons of ballast water containing potential invasive species, and toxic by-products from dry cleaning and photo labs. There are more than 120 cruise ships of this size operating around the world, plus 100 smaller ships. Currently, these ships can dump their untreated sewage anywhere beyond three miles from shore and are not required to treat gray water or ballast water before dumping.

Both the Pew Oceans Commission and the president's U.S. Commission on Ocean Policy have highlighted cruise ship pollution as a problem we can and must solve on the path to sustainable, healthy oceans. In response, I joined Sen. Richard J. Durbin, D-Ill., to introduce the Clean Cruise Ship Act. Our bill closes loopholes in the Clean Water Act and prohibits cruise ships from discharging sewage, gray water and bilge within 12 miles of our coast. Plus, it requires any waste dumped beyond this zone to be treated. The bill mandates

A Flood of Waste

BIG GROWTH

- **5 million** Number of North Americans taking a cruise in 1996

- **10 million** Number of North Americans taking cruises in 2006

- **47%** Increase in cruise passengers [from 2001 to 2006]

BIG POLLUTION

- **5 to 7 gallons** Sewage dumped per passenger per day

- **420 million gallons** Sewage dumped per year

- **3 miles** Distance from shore where raw sewage is dumped

- **0 miles** Distance from shore where treated sewage and raw graywater is dumped

Bluewater Network, 2006.

regular inspections of discharge operations and equipment and creates a three-year program where onboard observers would guarantee compliance.[1]

Some within the industry argue that their voluntarily adopted waste-management protocols are sufficient, making the Clean Cruise Ship Act redundant. Unfortunately, their "trust us, we won't pollute" line has not held up in practice.

1. Both S. 793 and HR 1636, which would have constituted the Clean Cruise Ship Act, died in committee.

In one case, a cruise line that had a voluntary agreement not to dump waste in the Monterey Bay National Marine Sanctuary dumped 36,000 gallons of gray water, treated bilge and black water into the sanctuary—and only admitted to it five months later after a direct inquiry by regulators. Why didn't the company admit to the dump? Because it "wasn't illegal, only a violation of a voluntary policy."

Cruise ships carry over 8 million passengers to and through our nation's most beautiful and fragile marine ecosystems annually. We have the technology to ensure that these visits do not leave behind harmful wastes—let's make sure we're using it.

"*[Cruise lines] work diligently to eliminate all forms of pollution through improved environmental policies, procedures and technology.*"

Voluntary Efforts Are Adequate to Reduce Cruise Ship Pollution

Michael Crye

*Most cruise lines voluntarily maintain rigorous waste manage-
ment standards to protect the marine environment, claims
Michael Crye in the following viewpoint. In fact, he asserts, the
survival of the cruise industry depends on preserving the natural
beauty of the environment, which for many is a central part of
the cruise experience. He maintains, for example, that the Cruise
Lines International Association (CLIA) waste management standards meet and exceed domestic and international environmental laws. Indeed, Crye argues, CLIA ships employ the latest technology to minimize waste. Crye is executive vice-president of
CLIA.*

Michael Crye, "A Delicate Balance," *World Cruise Industry Review*, March 1, 2007.
Copyright © 2007 SPG Media Limited, a subsidiary of SPG Media Group PLC. Reproduced by permission.

As you read, consider the following questions:

1. What are some of the environmental challenges facing every segment of the maritime industry, in Crye's opinion?

2. To what does the author claim coral reefs are particularly sensitive?

3. According to Crye, what will the Blue Cruise Programme accomplish?

The cruise industry is continually exploring ways to foster and gauge its success, as well as to correct its deficits. Although cruise comprises less than 5% of all passenger ships and only 0.2% of the world's merchant fleet, it leads the way in cutting-edge technology and management practices that foster a healthy marine environment.

Facing Environmental Challenges

The environmental challenges facing cruise are the same environmental challenges facing every segment of the maritime industry:

- *Air emissions* on cruise ships are being addressed with cruise industry support for the development and introduction of new engines that dramatically reduce air emissions. In addition, the development of innovative enviroengines has resulted in emission reductions as well as less fuel use and no visible smoke.

- *Ballast water and non-native species* are the bane of ship operators worldwide, but the cruise industry is taking every feasible step to curb the problem. First of all, cruise ships travel to open ocean environments to take on their ballast water, so the chances of taking on non-native species are reduced. In addition, the industry is testing a number of new technologies, including the use of ozone, ultraviolet, filtration, heat, chemical brocides and deoxygenation to help reduce this problem. At the same time, the US Environmental Protection Agency (EPA) is working on 22 potential approaches to assist in finding a solution.

- *Wastewater* includes both greywater, the largest form of liquid waste and the by-product of cleaning, and blackwater, which is sewage. The industry has agreed to discharge greywater and blackwater only when ships are underway at a speed of not less than six knots and are more than four miles away from port. In addition, marine sanitation devices are used to process blackwater with discharge characteristics equivalent to land-side treatment plants. Some Cruise Lines International Association (CLIA) members have adopted even stricter rules and continue to develop new advanced treatment systems that produce quality drinking water from effluent that should eventually be permitted to be discharged anywhere.

- *Hazardous waste* is of great concern to the members of the CLIA. The Waste Management Practices and Procedures, which have been agreed to by all CLIA members, are very specific. These standards require the disposal of all hazardous materials by licensed land-side vendors who must ensure full compliance with laws and environmental regulations. In addition, operators are eliminating the use of products that result in the production of hazardous waste materials. Where products cannot be eliminated, procedures are being put in place to limit their use.

- *Oily bilge water* is the result of minor engine and machinery leaks, as well as residue from maintenance. Management of oily bilge water is a challenge the cruise industry takes very seriously. In addition to the current generation of oily water separators resulting in

One Cruise Line's Commitment

1. We treat all sewage with marine sanitation devices certified by the U.S. Coast Guard, and discharge far from
   shore.
2. We do not dump trash overboard.
3. We do not dispose of toxic chemicals at sea.
4. We are closely monitored and inspected by independent,
   outside environmental auditors.

Richard D. Fain, Royal Caribbean Cruises Ltd.

lower oil content in discharge, the introduction of new technology, such as gas turbine engines and the use of plasma energy to treat bilge water, now makes it possible to reach environmental goals that were not possible a decade ago.

Coral reefs are one of the most wondrous spectacles in the world and are particularly sensitive to oily bilge. These delicate reefs are home to many species of fish and are an important source of pharmaceutical compounds. Diseased or damaged reefs are a detriment to the cruise business as well as the planet's environment. CLIA members have gone to great lengths to promote their growth and well-being through strict practices and procedures in and around the reefs, as well as advocacy and support of education and research to enhance their survival.

Addressing the Challenges

From technology to procedures to programmes, the cruise industry is ready to work with other responsible parties to protect and promote a clean environment worldwide. CLIA's commitment, both in terms of money and manpower, to making this happen is second only to its determination to ensure that CLIA members uphold the standards agreed upon in the mandatory Waste Management Practices and Procedures, which meets or exceeds environmental laws worldwide. Recent environmental awards to CLIA member lines are a testament to the industry commitment to the health of the planet.

Separate studies by the EPA and Science Advisory Panel of the State of Alaska showed that wastewater from cruise ships was dispersed quickly with minimal impact on the marine environment. In July 2002, the Alaska Department of Environmental Conservation (ADEC) conducted Whole Effluent Toxicity (WET) tests on the wastewater effluent from five different cruise ships operating in Alaskan waters.

In these WET-testing cases, the short- and long-term lethal or reproductive effects on indigenous marine animal species were examined in various dilutions of discharge streams from cruise ships. Study results show that at a dilution rate of 200:1, wastewater has almost no impact on the animal species. The ADEC scientific review panel stated that wastewater discharges from large cruise ships, while underway, are not of immediate concern.

Preserving Natural Beauty

The natural beauty seen from a cruise ship reminds everyone of the duty to be faithful stewards of the environment. Whether this means taking in the sight of a delicate coral reef in the Caribbean or gazing at the majestic glaciers of Alaska, pristine water and crystal-clear skies represent an essential component of the overall cruise experience.

CLIA cruise lines are committed to preserving and protecting the environment because their success and survival depends on it. The CLIA and its member lines work diligently to eliminate all forms of pollution through improved environmental policies, procedures and technology. CLIA members have adopted aggressive programmes of waste minimisation, waste reuse and recycling, waste stream management and shore-side waste disposal. In addition, the cruise lines have invested millions of dollars in technology to continuously improve the environmental performance of their vessels.

These measures are not only intended to ensure compliance with the domestic and international laws that govern shipboard operations, they are also vital to preserving the waters in which all cruise ships sail and the ports they visit. In addition to these programmes, the CLIA is committed to preserving environmental resources by ensuring that all member cruise lines adhere to its Cruise Industry Waste Management Practices and Procedures.

Cruise ships are regulated by both international treaties and domestic law regarding safety and pollution prevention. This is necessary due to the variety of jurisdictional locations that a cruise ship might enter during a typical cruise.

Waste Management Standards

CLIA member cruise vessel operators have incorporated the following areas into standards for waste stream management:

- Greywater and blackwater discharge

- Bilge and oily water residues

- Photo processing disposal, including X-ray development fluid

- Dry-cleaning fluid disposal

- Print shop waste fluid disposal

- Photocopying and laser printer cartridge recycling

- Unused and outdated pharmaceutical disposal

- Fluorescent and mercury vapour lamp bulbs disposal

- Battery recycling

- Glass, cardboard, aluminum and steel can recycling

- Handling of incinerator ash

International and federal regulations provide an environmentally sound operation. However, the standards adopted by the CLIA and its members in July 2001 marked the first time in history that an association of international passenger vessel operators agreed to adhere to a wide range of waste management practices and procedures, many of which go beyond the requirements of the international and US regulatory agencies.

These environmental standards are stringent and comprehensive. They are not only intended to ensure compliance with the laws that govern ship-board operations, they are also necessary for preserving the waters on which cruise vessels sail.

The cruise industry recognises that it is important to be well received in the communities in which it does business. With that comes a certain responsibility that cruise ships do not leave a place less desirable than they found it. The CLIA pledges to do its part to protect nature's delicate resources.

> *"Research has provided support for the concept of ocean fertilization as a viable means to sequester carbon dioxide for hundreds to about a thousand years."*

Ocean Iron Fertilization May Reduce Global Warming's Impact

Dan Whaley, Margaret Leinen, and Kevin Whilden

Carbon dioxide (CO_2) is removed from the atmosphere by plants during photosynthesis, a process known as carbon sequestration. When CO_2-consuming marine plants such as phytoplankton sink, they export carbon to the deep ocean. Fertilizing the ocean with iron to increase the growth of CO_2-consuming phytoplankton may reduce global warming, assert Dan Whaley, Margaret Leinen, and Kevin Whilden in the following viewpoint. Some critics claim that ocean iron fertilization (OIF) is illegal "dumping" or that it will have an adverse effect on the oceans, but such claims are unwarranted, the authors maintain. The purpose of OIF is to reduce the impact of climate change, not to dump waste, the authors claim. Moreover, they argue, no evidence sug-

Dan Whaley, Margaret Leinen, and Kevin Whilden, "Recent Critique of Ocean Iron Fertilization Rests on Flawed Interpretation of Data," CLIMOS Policy Response, December 19, 2007. © 2007 CLIMOS. Reproduced by permission.

gests that moderate OIF projects will damage the marine environment. Whaley and Whilden are founders of CLIMOS, and Leinen oversees scientific research for CLIMOS, an OIF company.

As you read, consider the following questions:

1. According to Whaley, Leinen, and Whilden, how does the University of Miami press release contrast with the findings of the Lutz et al. paper?

2. How do laws of the sea define "dumping," in the authors' view?

3. In the authors' opinion, why is the sale of carbon credits not fraudulent?

[The year] 2007 has seen an increase in the discussion of ocean iron fertilization as a method to sequester carbon dioxide in the deep ocean. New research has provided support for the concept of ocean fertilization as a viable means to sequester carbon dioxide for hundreds to about a thousand years. The press coverage of these papers has been minimal, which is not surprising, though some have found a wider audience. A recent paper by Lutz et al. published in October 2007 generated a curious press release more than a month after its publication. This University of Miami press release, titled "100 Billion Dollar Global Warming 'Fix' Discredited by New Research," claims ocean fertilization is a process that doesn't work. However, the statements in the press release related to lack of sequestration are contradicted by the findings in the very paper upon which it is based. Unfortunately this press release is starting to generate articles in the general media that incorrectly reference the scholarly paper as evidence that ocean fertilization is not a viable process to sequester atmospheric carbon dioxide into the deep ocean.

The paper by Dr. Michael Lutz, Ken Caldeira, Robert Dunbar, and Michael Behrenfeld, is titled "Seasonal rhythms of net primary production and particulate organic carbon flux to depth describe the efficiency of biological pump in the global ocean." This very interesting paper synthesizes the results from hundreds of sediment trap deployments to estimate particulate organic carbon flux throughout the world's oceans. Sediment traps are a direct observational record of the biological pump in exporting carbon into the deep ocean. The paper calculates seasonal variations or carbon export, and develops a relationship between the fluxes and estimates of total surface ocean net primary productivity (NPP) inferred from satellite data. This is an interesting approach to gauging the biological pump's overall effectiveness in sequestering atmospheric carbon into the deep ocean, and leverages the more broadly available NPP data as a proxy calibrated by sparser sediment trap data.

The Findings

The paper finds the following:

1. Carbon export at depth is greatest during the season of peak phytoplankton bloom. Also the relative difference in sequestration between peak and non-peak bloom increases towards Polar oceans. The paper found that in Polar oceans, "summertime fluxes to shallow, intermediate, and deep-water depths are 20, 10, and 5 times wintertime fluxes," and in Equatorial oceans, "seasons of maximum flux are generally double the rate of seasons of minimum flux."

2. The *ratio* of carbon export to Net Primary Productivity (NPP) decreases during peak bloom seasons, with the greatest reduction occurring in Polar oceans. This does not contradict the finding that the absolute value of carbon export is greater during peak bloom conditions, but does suggest that some mechanism reduces the *fraction* of carbon export from total phytoplankton biomass. Mechanisms proposed are increased predation on phytoplankton by zooplankton and other animals, and the increased decomposition of phytoplankton.

The Science of Ocean Fertilization

When sprinkled in the form of shavings, iron spurs a bloom of fast-growing plankton that soaks up carbon dioxide as it photosynthesizes. When it decomposes, the algae sinks deep into ocean waters, carrying the carbon with it. Drop enough iron, in theory, and the ocean becomes a vast greenhouse gas–absorbing machine.

Melanie Haiken, Business 2.0, *June 2007.*

This is a meaningful paper in the field of ocean fertilization–related literature. The comprehensive summary of sediment trap data segregated by seasonality is unique and new. The comparison of biological productivity with carbon export greatly increases our understanding or the "geobiological dynamics" behind the most effective natural mechanism for removing CO_2 from the atmosphere (e.g., the biological pump).

A Faulty Interpretation

In contrast, the press release by the University of Miami Rosenstiel School of Marine & Atmospheric Science, makes the following statements based on the paper described above:

1. "Research performed at Stanford and Oregon State Universities suggests that ocean fertilization may not be an effective method of reducing carbon dioxide in the atmosphere."

2. "[The researchers] found clear seasonal patterns in both algal abundance and carbon sinking rates. However, the relationship between the two was surprising: less carbon was transported to deep water during a summertime bloom than during the rest of the year."

3. "Indeed, the global study of Dr. Lutz and colleagues suggests that greatly enhanced carbon sequestration should

not be expected no matter the location or duration of proposed large-scale ocean fertilization experiments."

These statements are clearly not consistent with the Lutz et al. paper, which demonstrates a 2–20 fold *increase* in total carbon sequestration during peak phytoplankton bloom events throughout the world's oceans. Statements 2 and 3 appear to be based on a faulty interpretation of the difference between absolute vs. relative variations in seasonal sequestration rates. Rather than providing evidence that iron fertilization doesn't work, the paper provides strong support that ocean iron fertilization projects are likely to generate increased carbon sequestration, particularly in high latitude oceans.

Answering the Critics

The Press Release also quotes Professor Rosemary Rayfuse of the University of New South Wales who makes several incorrect statements:

> 1. "Ocean fertilization is 'dumping' which is essentially prohibited under the law of the sea."

First, OIF is not dumping. "Dumping" is defined under the relevant international agreements to include "any deliberate disposal" into the sea of "wastes or other matter from vessels," but to exclude "placement of matter for a purpose other than the mere disposal thereof, provided that such placement is not contrary to the aims of [the agreement]." Because any iron used in an ocean fertilization project is obviously placed in the ocean for a purpose other than disposal, ocean fertilization could be treated as "dumping" only if it were deemed contrary to the aims of the relevant agreement. Given the threats that climate change poses to oceans and marine ecosystems and the important role that iron fertilization could play in slowing those adverse impacts, iron fertilization projects are fully consistent with the aims of relevant international instruments, *provided that such projects are appropriately designed and executed so that they pose a minimum risk of adverse impacts on ocean ecosystems.* Projects that meet those criteria would therefore not be treated as "dumping" under these agreements.

Even if a particular OIF project were to fall within the scope of the "dumping" definition, moreover, it would not be prohibited under the law of the sea. The Law of the Sea Convention does not prohibit dumping but instead essentially imports the legal framework for dumping that is established under a specialized agreement called the London Convention. Nor does the London Convention itself prohibit dumping: Instead it imposes a permit requirement. Indeed, the most recent Meeting of the Consultative Parties to the London Convention, while urging caution with respect to OIF projects and concluding that large-scale OIF projects were "not currently justified" based on its state of knowledge at that time, recognized that "it is within the purview of each state to consider proposals on a case-by-case." The Parties neither concluded that OIF should be treated as "dumping" nor interpreted OIF as prohibited under the Convention.

Exaggerated, Inaccurate Claims

2. "There is no point trying to ameliorate the effects of climate change by destroying the oceans—the very cradle of life on earth. Simply doing more and bigger of that which has already been demonstrated to be ineffective and potentially more harmful than good is counter-intuitive at best."

Although concerns have been raised about impacts of ocean iron fertilization, there is no scientific evidence of deleterious effects of ocean fertilization that suggests it is capable of "destroying the oceans." Evidence from the present and from the last million years suggests this will not happen. Tens of millions of tons of iron from atmospheric dust fertilize the ocean naturally every year, and are a necessary component of fundamental biologic functioning of the ocean. Furthermore,

Ice Ages have been shown to have 4–8 times greater iron flux than current conditions, and this has been linked to large-scale removals or CO_2 from the atmosphere. Finally, significant biological benefits have been seen in some instances of natural iron fertilization, and the Lutz et al. paper also suggests this is a possibility.

> 3. ". . . ocean fertilization projects are not currently approved under any carbon credit regulatory scheme and the sale of offsets or credits from ocean fertilization on the unregulated voluntary markets is basically nothing short of fraudulent."

This hyperbole is also inaccurate. It is true that ocean fertilization has not been submitted for approval under any existing regulatory framework, however this does not make the sale of such credits in the general carbon market fraudulent. Ocean fertilization carbon credits should follow the rigorous protocols of methodologies and verification to prove that certified carbon credits are real, additional, and permanent. The voluntary carbon market is a large worldwide market for many project categories which fall outside of currently accepted regulatory frameworks. Important new techniques such as Carbon Capture and Storage, Avoided Deforestation, Afforestation/Reforestation, and others are excellent examples of large-scale carbon mitigation techniques which are currently funded via these mechanisms and which are by no means fraudulent simply because they lie outside regulatory frameworks.

Scientific evidence suggests that ocean iron fertilization projects can be increased to a moderate scale without any fear of negative ecological consequences, and recent peer-reviewed scientific literature and science press have demonstrated substantial support for these further demonstrations. The Lutz et al. paper provides evidence for greater total flux of carbon to the deep ocean during phytoplankton blooms. We believe that it is unfortunate that the University of Miami press release incorrectly characterizes the results of this high quality research. We would encourage them to strive for a more factual and balanced tone in the future.

> "Ocean fertilization cannot reverse or even stanch the increase of atmospheric CO_2."

Ocean Iron Fertilization Will Not Reduce Global Warming's Impact

Andrew Myers

While global warming is a serious problem, fertilizing the oceans with iron—which some believe will increase CO_2-consuming marine plants—is not the solution, argues Andrew Myers in the following viewpoint. No evidence demonstrates that ocean iron fertilization (OIF) will reverse the increase in CO_2, he maintains. Moreover, Myers claims, the adverse impact on the world's oceans could be significant: the increase in phytoplankton will likely reduce deep ocean oxygen, and the organisms that eat the phytoplankton may emit harmful gases such as methane. Myers is editor of Ocean Conservancy *magazine.*

As you read, consider the following questions:

1. According to Myers, under what conditions was the "iron hypothesis" first posited?

2. In the author's view, what are some of the consequences of global climate change?

3. Under what conditions might ocean iron fertilization be employed, in the author's opinion?

Sometime in early April of 2001, a breeze swirled in the Gobi Desert. As it twisted and rolled over the ancient, desiccated land it swept up grains of soil and carried them aloft into the skies. The breeze then grew into a full-fledged dust storm large enough that NASA [National Aeronautics and Space Administration] satellites began to take note. A day later, a khaki cloud moved over Japan and by April 12 ripples from the storm were first felt at Ocean Station PAPA at 50 degrees north latitude, 145 degrees west longitude in a swath of the north Pacific somewhere west of Alaska.

There, dust fell into the seas. A frisson of phytoplankton sprung to life. And, it grew. And, it grew some more. What happened at Ocean Station PAPA added an important piece to a theoretical puzzle scientists had been debating since at least 1989 when "Johnny Ironseed"—Dr. John Martin, director of the Moss Landing Marine Laboratory—first posited the "iron hypothesis" that terrestrial dust, borne by the winds, fertilizes aquatic plants that, in turn, check the level of carbon dioxide in the atmosphere.

The science behind this natural process operates on the tiniest scale. But, as some commercial interests quickly latched on to, the implication was potentially huge on another. Martin's iron hypothesis, they claimed, held nothing less than an answer to the problem of greenhouse gases filling the skies.

Life Out of Balance

Planet Earth and all that is hers—the land, the air and the water—acts as a single, integrated system of chemical checks and balances; a zero-sum game. You can't change one without affecting the others. Nonetheless, while most people think of global climate change as solely an atmospheric phenomenon, the oceans and the land are where the suffering is actually felt.

The debate about whether global climate change is occurring is no longer really a debate. Even the skeptics, what few of them there are, have conceded the point, although they look to the lower end of the accepted predictions and say the effects will be negligible. In the middle, there is plenty of wiggle room and the result is a political stalemate about what to do. The end-product, unfortunately, may be an inexorable march to catastrophe.

While there is debate over consequences and much that we don't know about global climate change, one thing we do know is that atmospheric carbon dioxide levels have risen sharply in the past 150 years, from 280 parts-per-million (ppm) to approximately 380 ppm today. To the total, we are adding another 1.5 ppm each year. That may not seem like much, but scenarios say we could see levels of 700 ppm or more in the not-too-distant future, almost triple the historical average. Carbon dioxide traps heat in the atmosphere. More CO_2 means more heat, ergo global climate change.

The Weight of the World

For the oceans, the potential consequences of global climate change are serious and many. Truth be told, the oceans are among the earth's systems most affected by global temperature fluctuation. Devastating coral bleaching episodes are now occurring due, at least in part, to warmer water temperatures. Species are shifting their ranges as tropical marine wildlife move to new areas that were once too cold for them. More severe, and perhaps more frequent, hurricanes are likely on the horizon, as well. And then there is the specter that melting glaciers may pour enough fresh water into the ocean to lower the salinity of seawater—slowing, if not stopping, the crucial ocean currents that regulate global temperatures and deliver much needed nutrients from the depths to the upper layers of the oceans.

One serious prediction that has become reality is ocean acidification, a result of carbon dioxide dissolving in the water. Since the start of the industrial age, seawater has grown slightly more acidic, a process that will continue for the foreseeable future. Adding 200 years of current emissions to the oceans would effectively double the acid in the water. Eventually, acidification will have a profound impact on all marine life that rely upon calcium carbonate to build shells and skeletons. Bedrock species of coral and plankton, species that anchor the ocean's food web, will literally dissolve in the waters that once sustained them.

Sea level rise is another serious threat. The increase in water levels, from both glacial melting and the physical expansion that occurs naturally as water warms, has been approximately a half-foot in the last century. Conservative estimates say a rise of another half-foot to a foot-and-a-half is likely—a troubling but manageable increase. More dire scenarios say the seas may rise three feet or more over the next century. The concomitant flooding could inundate important river deltas, wetlands, atolls and shorelines. The waters would threaten arable or inhabited land, including some major population centers and low-lying island nations. Tens-of-millions of people would be affected worldwide.

These are grim factors all, if they prove out.

Cause du Jour

When scientists talk of controlling carbon dioxide they are trying to find ways to keep it out of the skies for a long time, eons preferably. Trees are a form of carbon storage, they take in CO_2 and convert it to organic matter. The oceans, too, harbor carbon. In fact, next to limestone, the oceans are the biggest carbon repository on earth. It is estimated that the oceans already hold 39,000 billion tons of carbon. By comparison, the atmosphere now contains just 750 billion tons. So great is the oceans' capacity that if all the carbon dioxide in the atmosphere were dissolved in the oceans, the concentration would increase by less than two percent.

So it happened that John Martin's theory, the "Geritol solution," became the cause du jour in the clamor to mitigate the damage humans are causing through the burning of fossil fuels. What Martin realized was that phytoplankton—tiny floating marine plants after all—need basic nutrients for life, among them nitrogen, phosphorus, silicon, and iron. Certain areas of the oceans, while rich in most of those nutrients, lack the trace amounts of iron necessary to spark plant life. There are huge expanses of these high nutrient, low chlorophyll (HNLC) waters in the northern and equatorial Pacific and, especially, in the Southern Ocean surrounding Antarctica. And, while phytoplankton account for just one percent of the living matter on earth, they absorb almost the same amount of CO_2 as all of the plants on land combined. What's more, ocean fertilization tests have shown blooms generated through ocean fertilization can produce 20- or even 30-fold increases in phytoplankton very quickly.

So, the theory goes, if we were to perpetually sprinkle iron over these ostensibly dead waters, phytoplankton would bloom. They, in turn, would absorb copious amounts of CO_2 then die and sink to the deep ocean where they—and the carbon they contain—would remain for many decades, if not millennia as some have speculated. If Martin were right about phytoplankton and carbon fixation, something on the order of 100,000 atoms of carbon would be sequestered for every one atom of iron stirred into the ocean—an astounding uptake factor. So astounding, in fact, that Martin stated boldly, "Give me half a tanker of iron and I'll give you the next ice age."

It doesn't take a climatologist to fathom the potential: more phytoplankton mean less carbon dioxide. It wasn't long

Ecological Concerns

Large-scale iron fertilization, in altering the base of the food chain, might lead to undesirable changes in fish stocks and whale populations. Increased decomposition of sinking organic matter could deprive deep waters of oxygen or produce other greenhouse gases more potent than carbon dioxide, such as nitrous oxide and methane. The plankton-choked surface waters could block sunlight needed by deeper corals, or warm the surface layer and change circulation patterns.

Hugh Powell, Oceanus, *November 2007.*

before the scientific community and the geoengineers were looking seriously to the oceans for an answer to global climate change. Then, in 1997, the Kyoto Protocols set out a worldwide agreement for the voluntary reduction of greenhouse gas emissions. Under Kyoto, CO_2 emissions are capped for each country through a yearly system of credits. Polluters who use all their credits can buy more from those who haven't. Suddenly, there was money to be made. The Department of Energy, even the behemoths of the energy industry, began to take note.

Science Has Its Say

Could the answer to greenhouse gases really be as simple as fertilizing a desolate stretch of the Antarctic ocean with common, everyday iron? While most scientists agree that ocean fertilization could work to a degree, it will never be the cure the commercial enterprises have promised. One key question is just how much of the carbon would actually make it to the deep ocean, for only there does it remain long enough to be environmentally effective. As experiments have shown, most of the carbon trapped in the dead phytoplankton is converted back to CO_2 through decay in the water column—going right back where it came from very quickly; zero effect. Best estimates are that only perhaps one percent or less of all carbon taken up through photosynthesis in open-ocean surface waters makes it to the bottom.

In 2005, Richard E. Zeebe of the University of Hawaii, and David Archer of the University of Chicago, used various scientific computer models to show that even if 20 percent of the oceans were fertilized 15 times per year for 100 years, the expected reduction of CO_2 in the atmosphere would be approximately 15 ppm, and that from levels expected to reach 700 ppm or more by the year 2100. Recall that 70 percent of the earth's surface is ocean, so we are talking about fertilizing 14 percent of the surface of the entire planet, 15 times a year, for the next century to accomplish a reduction that would have very little impact on carbon dioxide levels.

So, though all the science indicates that ocean fertilization cannot reverse or even stanch the increase of atmospheric CO_2, some commercial entities, with much to gain, are intent on propagating the idea. To do so, they will, by the very definition of ocean fertilization, fundamentally alter our ocean ecosystems in order to do it. "The track record of humans in predicting the effect of large-scale ecological manipulations (including intentional introduction of species for biological control) is not at all good," says John Cullen, Killam Chair in Ocean Studies at Dalhousie University in Halifax, Nova Scotia. "It has been clearly shown that large scale ocean fertilization, operating at maximum efficiency—something that is unlikely to be possible—could not stop projected increases of atmospheric CO_2," he says. At best, he concedes, "ocean fertilization will merely delay the projected increases by several years."

Truth and Consequences

And then, there are the side effects. Deep ocean hypoxia (low oxygen levels) or even anoxia (no oxygen) will likely occur, caused by decaying phytoplankton. Or, microbial communities at the bottom of the ocean, those which feed on the dead plankton, might emit other, more harmful gases like methane and nitrous oxide. Conversion of carbon to methane, with 21 times the heat trapping effect of CO_2, might actually make global climate change worse. Even the phytoplankton themselves have been shown to emit environmentally harmful gases like isoprene, dimethyl sulfide and others. Isoprene, an important precursor to ozone, increased four times in one experiment. Dimethyl sulfide might seed cloud formation, which would limit the amount of light reaching the water thus reducing the effectiveness of fertilization over time. And, of course, there's the lingering question of acidification, which will certainly grow worse with increases in dissolved CO_2 content of deep waters.

"We can predict deep ocean acidification and reduced oxygen, with numerous potential consequences that could offset the hypothetical benefits of fertilization," Cullen says flatly.

Mark Lawrence, an atmospheric scientist at the Max Planck Institute for Chemistry in Mainz, Germany, agrees and goes a step farther. "These are the consequences we currently know about, what about those we can't even predict yet? The potential for negative impacts, both known and unknown, appears to be particularly large for ocean iron fertilization, especially when compared to other geoengineering possibilities discussed thus far."

Back to the Drawing Board

Even those in the scientific community who support ocean fertilization sound a cautious note. Only as a last resort should ocean fertilization contribute and then as just one of a laundry list of other efforts to rein in greenhouse gases, a list topped by—you guessed it—reducing our reliance on fossil fuels. "In an imperfect world where we fail to stop using fossil fuels, ocean fertilization could help. But, it's not the whole solution. It's not a panacea," adds Dr. Kenneth Johnson, of the Monterey Bay Marine Research Institute, among those in favor of keeping ocean fertilization on the table. "The real answer is to ramp down carbon dioxide emissions to a sustainable level."

Others see it more simply. "The ocean has been proposed as a dumping ground of last resort for all sorts of human waste—everything from nuclear wastes to household trash—based on the idea that the ocean can absorb anything. Ocean fertilization is just another form of waste disposal," noted Mark Powell, an oceanographer and Director of Fish Conservation at The Ocean Conservancy. "Let's not trade the hell we know for the one we don't."

Amen.

| "By eschewing [the Law of the Sea Convention] treaty that almost all nations follow, the United States undermines its leadership in oceans policy."

The United States Should Ratify the UN Convention on the Law of the Sea

Benjamin Friedman and Daniel Friedman

In the following viewpoint, Benjamin Friedman and Daniel Friedman assert that to protect its maritime interests and restore the world's oceans to health, the United States must ratify the UN Convention on the Law of the Sea. The treaty poses no threat to American sovereignty, they claim. Indeed, the authors reason, failure to sign the treaty would subject the United States to the decisions of tribunals on which it has no voice. Signing the treaty does not threaten national security; in fact, the treaty helps stop nuclear proliferation, they maintain. The authors prepared this viewpoint for the Bipartisan Security Group, a think tank of Democratic and Republican experts.

Benjamin Friedman and Daniel Friedman, "How the Law of the Sea Convention Benefits the United States," Bipartisan Security Group, November 2004. Reproduced by permission.

As you read, consider the following questions:

1. Why does the U.S. Navy support the convention, according to the Friedmans?

2. In the authors' view, how does the convention protect U.S. environmental interests?

3. How is the Continental Shelf Commission crucial to the U.S. energy industry and supply, in the Friedmans' opinion?

O pponents [of the Law of the Sea Convention] argue that the Convention should be rejected because Ronald Reagan refused to sign it in 1982. They argue that it poses risks to national security. They argue that acceding to the Convention would cede U.S. sovereignty to international organizations. These claims are baseless. By signing the Convention, the United States would enhance its ability to project military power and fight nuclear proliferation. It would protect shipping lanes and fishing rights, win offshore mining rights, claim exclusive access to all marine resources up to 200 miles off its coast, and protect its environment. By failing to ratify the Convention, the United States forgoes these benefits. It loses its place at the table on several international committees that will determine the policies that govern the seas. And by eschewing a treaty that almost all nations follow, the United States undermines its leadership in oceans policy and beyond. . . .

National Security

The Navy is a primary supporter of the Convention because it ensures the right of free passage. Naval leaders have repeatedly argued that American power depends on the ability to move without inhibition across the world's oceans—the ability to project power. Much of America's military might is naval. American nuclear submarines, aircraft carriers, and every other naval vessel must pass along coastlines and through narrow straits and archipelagos. American planes also rely on free passage to pass above coastal waters of foreign states.

Each year the United States challenges dozens of states for asserting legal rights that impede freedom of the seas. Iran, North Korea, and China have all challenged the U.S. Navy's free passage through their EEZ [exclusive economic zone]. By codifying the right to pass freely through the exclusive economic zone of foreign states without restrictions on cargo or formation, the Law of the Sea strengthens America's ability to project power.

But these rights are already recognized as customary international law. What does the Convention add? For one, it makes these rights stronger. Written treaties are perceived as more powerful than customary laws. By signing the Convention, the United States gives added weight and stability to customary rights, and pushes recalcitrant states to respect navigational freedoms.

More importantly, the Convention creates a forum to change navigational rights. It is possible, though unlikely, that future deliberations under the Convention might create rules that undermine freedom of navigation. If the United States fails to ratify the Convention, it will lose the opportunity to defend these rights. The problem is not that other states can stop the U.S. Navy from sailing where they want to sail. The problem is that they can raise the costs of doing so. If a nation decides to forbid U.S. ships their legal right to pass, America could use force to assert our right. But, realistically, it will be more likely to seek legal remedy. Signing the Convention lowers the cost of projecting power.

Helping Stop Proliferation

The most absurd argument made against the Convention is the notion that it would hinder U.S. efforts to interdict shipments of materials used for nuclear, chemical and biological weapons and the missiles used to deliver them. The opposite is true. Signing the Convention helps stop proliferation.

Opponents contend that because the Convention protects freedom of the seas and freedom of passage in territorial waters, signing would prohibit the U.S. Navy from stopping suspect shipments. This argument is based on a misunderstanding of both international law and America's current nonproliferation efforts. The Convention offers states limited reasons for violating a ship's freedom of the seas or right of innocent passage, and these reasons do not include carrying weapons. But these constraints on U.S. conduct already exist. Freedom of the seas and the right of innocent passage are codified in the treaties the United States passed in 1958 and subsequently recognized as customary international law. If the United States ever had a right to stop shipments without regard for freedom of the seas and the right of innocent passage, that right is long gone. The Convention imposes no new restrictions on the United States' ability to interdict weapons shipments. . . .

The Environmental Protections

The overwhelming support of environmental groups demonstrates that the Convention aids U.S. environmental interests. The Convention is partially an effort to prevent depletion of the global commons and avoid classic collective action problems that lead to the destruction of goods that have both inherent value and value to businesses. For instance, the Convention contains provisions to control overfishing and protect fishing rights. Existing vessel safety and pollution accords depend on the Convention, and the Convention's rules will be the basis for future agreements. The Convention establishes the principle that states have both the right to use the oceans and obligations to do so without sullying it. As a party to the Convention, the United States will be in a stronger negotiating position on future environmental accords and will have more

Restoring Damaged Oceans

If the U.S. can't agree to engage in global ocean governance, how can it ever begin to address the complex and challenging task of restoring our damaged oceans to health? It's long past time to schedule the Law of the Sea vote, get our overdue homework done and improve our ocean policy grade.

David Helvarg, Los Angeles Times, *March 12, 2007.*

success in aiding enforcement of existing environmental obligations. The energy and shipping industries support the agreement as vociferously as the environmentalists, demonstrating that the Convention will not impose costly regulations on U.S. industry.

The Law of the Sea Convention opened for amendment in November, 2004. The need for ratification is urgent. While the United States stays outside the Convention, other states can start negotiating issues affecting U.S. interests in a forum where the United States is not represented. By not signing, the United States bars itself from the ISA [International Seabed Authority], the Law of the Sea Tribunal, and the Continental Shelf Commission. With 146 states adhering to the Convention, these bodies make policy that governs all states' relations at sea, affecting American interests whether or not the United States ratifies the treaty.

Participating in Governing Bodies

The ISA administers deep seabed mining. Without ratifying the treaty, the United States cannot capitalize on the changes it won in the ISA. Opponents of the Convention argue the ISA's power to administer the sea floor "supersedes the power of participating states." But the ISA was created because no state has sovereignty over the seabed. No one can own the sea floor. It remains a commons. As Senator [Richard] Lugar puts it, "The only way to establish legal norms in an area where no sovereignty exists is through international agreement." By clarifying the extent of national jurisdiction over coastal waters, the Law of the Sea Convention in fact strengthens state sovereignty.

The role of the Law of the Sea Tribunal is to resolve disputes over the Convention. The Convention mandates that the Tribunal resolve all disputes, except those involving military activities. Opponents of the Convention argue that the tribunal could dispute U.S. designations of certain activities as military, forcing the U.S. to limit military operations. Some even claim American "citizens could be dragged before politically motivated foreign jurists."

Professor John Norton Moore, the leading U.S. expert on the law of the sea, told the Senate Foreign Relations Committee that the chances of the Tribunal undermining U.S. military operations was comparable to that of a meteorite striking the capitol building. Still, administration officials have taken precautions. Upon joining the Convention, the United States would submit a declaration stipulating that it is acceding on the condition that states themselves have the authority to decide whether activities are military. Opponents think that even this precaution leaves a chance of the Tribunal harassing the U.S. military. As a party to the Convention, however, the United States can nominate the judges to sit on the tribunal, rendering this wildly remote possibility even more unlikely.

If the United States does not ratify the Convention, it has no control over the decisions the Tribunal reaches. The Tribunal will never have power over the U.S. military, but its decisions will form precedents that will help resolve future maritime disputes. Those precedents would affect U.S. interests.

Preventing Legal Uncertainties

The Continental Shelf Commission is crucial to the U.S. energy industry and supply. The Commission is a forum for states to register claims to extract materials from areas of their continental shelf. Today the United States obtains 28% of its natural gas and nearly as much oil from the Outer Continental Shelf. This amount will increase as technologies allow petroleum production in deeper waters—areas outside the 200 mile American exclusive economic zone that the Convention protects. To gain certainty to its rights to mine in these areas, the United States needs to submit claims to the Continental Shelf Commission, which will allow American companies to extract materials. These claims could expand U.S. areas for resource exploitation by 290,000 square miles. Without a legal claim, U.S. companies will face legal uncertainties, creating risks that undermine investment.

Moreover, there is competition for resources. Russia has already submitted a claim for areas in the Arctic that the United States might profitably mine. By staying out of the Convention, the United States loses it ability to submit claims to areas ripe for energy extraction and to help weigh claims others submit. The result is a massive lost opportunity to make money and increase domestic energy supply.

The United States cannot avoid the ISA, the Law of the Sea Tribunal, and the Continental Shelf Commission, but it can lead them. By joining Convention, the U.S. can regain its role, relinquished in 1982, as the leader of international efforts to establish the rule of law in the oceans. This would be a step toward the broader goal of repairing America's international standing. The [George W.] Bush Administration's foreign policy decisions have created the perception that the United States opposes the advancement of international law and cooperation. By joining the treaty, the United States could weaken this perception and begin reestablishing American leadership of international institutions.

The Law of the Sea is not a U.N. plan imposed on Americans by foreign bureaucrats. It is an international regime that the United States built to protect and assert its maritime interests. American power is not great enough to protect these interests without international cooperation. The treaty serves America. How then have a few radicals managed to impede it? In part by advancing claims, either through ignorance or deception, that are flat-out false. These claims will not fool anyone who spends any time studying the treaty. They are red herrings. They reflect not a rational analysis of the costs and benefits of joining the Convention, but a deep-seated, ideological opposition to any form of international cooperation.[1]

1. As of July 2008, the United States had not ratified the Law of the Sea Convention.

> *"[The Law of the Sea Treaty] would constitute the most egregious transfer of American sovereignty, wealth, and power to the U.N. since the founding of that 'world body.'"*

The United States Should Not Ratify the UN Convention on the Law of the Sea

Frank J. Gaffney Jr.

The United States should not ratify the UN Convention on the Law of the Sea Treaty (LOST) because the treaty would transfer U.S. sovereignty and wealth to the United Nations, argues Frank J. Gaffney Jr. in the following viewpoint. LOST creates an international organization with exceedingly broad control over how the ocean's resources will be used, he maintains. Moreover, the treaty could interfere with American national security initiatives, Gaffney claims. The United States should not submit to regulations that limit its ability to conduct counterterrorism efforts, he concludes. Gaffney contributes regularly to National Review, *a conservative biweekly news and opinion magazine.*

As you read, consider the following questions:

1. What president does Gaffney claim rejected the Law of the Sea Treaty?
2. Why does the author call the U.S. Navy's arguments favoring the treaty the River Kwai Syndrome?
3. In Gaffney's opinion, what will the International Seabed Authority enable the UN to impose?

The [George W.] Bush administration risks grievously blurring where it stands on the appropriate, limited role of the United Nations in determining our security and other interests with its advocacy of a treaty that President [Ronald] Reagan properly rejected [in 1982].... The administration's declared support for the Law of the Sea Treaty (LOST) caused it to be approved unanimously by the Senate Foreign Relations Committee—even though this accord would constitute the most egregious transfer of American sovereignty, wealth, and power to the U.N. since the founding of that "world body." In fact, never before in the history of the world has any nation voluntarily engaged in such a sweeping transfer to anyone.

This is the case because LOST creates a new supranational agency, the International Seabed Authority (ISA), which will have control of seven-tenths of the world surface area, i.e., the planet's international waters. That control will enable the ISA and a court created to adjudicate and enforce its edicts the right to determine who does what, where, when, and how in the oceans under its purview. This applies first and foremost to exploration and exploitation of the mineral and oil and gas deposits on or under the seabeds—an authority that will enable the U.N. for the first time to impose ... taxes on commercial activities.

American Sovereignty

LOST, however, will also interfere with America's sovereign exercise of freedom of the seas in ways that will have an adverse

Redistributing U.S. Wealth

[The Law of the Sea Treaty] is the globalists' dream bill. It would put the United States in a de facto world government that rules all the world's oceans under the pretense that they belong to "the common heritage of mankind." That's global-speak for allowing the United Nations and its affiliated organizations to carry out a massive, unprecedented redistribution of wealth from the United States to other countries.

Phyllis Schlafly, EagleForum.org, September 26, 2007.

effect on national security, especially in the post-9/11 world. Incredibly, it will preclude, for example, the president's important new Proliferation Security Initiative. PSI is a multinational arrangement whereby ships on the high seas that are suspected of engaging in the transfer of WMD [weapons of mass destruction]-related equipment can be intercepted, searched, and, where appropriate, seized. Its value was demonstrated in the recent interception of nuclear equipment headed to Libya.

Similarly, LOST will define intelligence collection in and submerged transit of territorial waters to be incompatible with the treaty's requirements that foreign powers conduct themselves in such seas only with "peaceful intent." The last thing we need is for some U.N. court—or U.S. lawyers in its thrall—to make it more difficult for us to conduct sensitive counterterrorism operations in the world's littorals. . . .

There have been several notable developments with respect to the Law of the Sea Treaty:

- It has become clear that one of the prime movers behind the Bush administration's support for this U.N.-

on-steroids treaty is none other than John Turner, a man property-rights activists kept from assuming a senior position in the Interior Department. Correctly seen by that community as a wild-eyed proponent of conservation at the expense of landowners' equities, he was given a consolation prize: a seemingly innocuous post as the State Department's assistant secretary for Oceans and International Environmental and Scientific Affairs. It turns out that in that position—and thanks to his longtime friendship with Vice President [Dick] Cheney—Turner has greatly advanced what is arguably the most egregious assault on property rights in history.

- The United States Navy has trotted out arguments for this treaty that reflect what might be called the River Kwai Syndrome. Like the British senior POW [prisoner of war] in World War II who couldn't bring himself to blow up a bridge his captors would use to their military advantage, Navy lawyers seem convinced that a bad deal is better than none.

- Even though this accord will manifestly interfere with important peacetime naval operations, JAG types [navy lawyers] tell us they think it will be good for their business if freedom of the seas is guaranteed by a new, U.N.-administered international legal system rather than by U.S. naval power. They speciously assert that a 1994 agreement negotiated by President [Bill] Clinton fixes the problems that caused President Reagan to reject LOST—never mind that the Clinton accord does not amend or otherwise formally modify one jot of the treaty. . . .

- Public scrutiny of the Law of the Sea Treaty will precipitate a time-consuming and politically costly debate [that] prompted [then] Senate Majority Leader Bill

Frist (R., Tenn.) to say that he sees no opportunity for the foreseeable future to bring this accord to the floor. Assuming he is good to his word, still more time will be available to awaken the American people to what is afoot.

- Most importantly, one of those people, President George W. Bush, may recently have been awakened to the dangers—political, as well as strategic and economic—inherent in this treaty. In response to a question . . . put to him by Paul Weyrich, the legendary conservative activist and president of the Free Congress Foundation, President Bush indicated that he was unaware of the Law of the Sea Treaty and his administration's support for it. It can only be hoped that, as he conducts the promised review of LOST, he will make clear he does not want it ratified, now or ever.

Better yet, President Bush should assign his [former] trusted undersecretary of Arms Control and International Security, John Bolton, the job of arranging for LOST to be "unsigned"—just as he did with respect to the fatally flawed treaty that created the International Criminal Court. Secretary Bolton would be particularly appropriate for this job, since he was also the prime architect of the Proliferation Security Initiative that the Law of the Sea Treaty would eviscerate.

While such developments are generally welcome, one thing curiously has not happened. The alarm about the defective Law of the Sea Treaty has still not been sounded by the likes of [conservative policy analyst] Rush Limbaugh and Fox News. It can only be hoped that . . . this oversight will be corrected, ensuring that the treaty is deep-sixed, once and for all.[1]

---

1. As of July 2008, the United States had not ratified the Law of the Sea Convention.

Periodical Bibliography

The following articles have been selected to supplement the diverse views presented in this chapter.

Economist	"Dolly Goes Swimming," July 19, 2007.
Frank J. Gaffney	"A L.O.S.T. Presidency," *Jewish World Review*, May 15, 2007.
Carol Gardner	"Making the Grade: An Ocean Agenda for the 110th Congress," *Ocean Conservancy*, Winter 2007.
Melanie Haiken	"Fertilizing Oceans for Fun and Profit," *Business 2.0*, June 2007.
David Helvarg	"Troubled Waters on U.N. Oceans Treaty," *Los Angeles Times*, March 12, 2007.
International Council of Cruise Lines	"The Cruise Industry: Committed to a Healthy Marine Environment," *World Cruise Industry Review*, 2007.
Ross A. Klein	"Attack of the Oversized Floating Playpen . . . Who Loses When You Go on Cruises?" *Briar Patch*, November 2006.
Margaret Leinen, Dan Whaley, and Kevin Whilden	"Are Carbon Offsets Appropriate for Ocean Iron Fertilization?" CLIMOS: Policy Response, January 28, 2008.
Hugh Powell	"Fertilizing the Ocean with Iron," *Oceanus*, November 2007.
Phyllis Schlafly	"Sink the Law of the Sea Again," Eagleforum .org, September 26, 2007, www.eagleforum.org/column/2007/sept07/07-09-26.html.
University of Southern California	"Sending Carbon Dioxide to Sea," *Science Daily*, January 13, 2008.

OPPOSING
VIEWPOINTS®
SERIES

CHAPTER 3

What Strategies Would Best Promote Sustainable Fishing?

Chapter Preface

Americans have been consuming genetically engineered corn and soybean products for some time. For farmers, genetically modified (GM) crops have the benefit of being resistant to pests or the toxic sprays that kill pests. Others maintain that because GM crops thrive under relatively harsh conditions, these crops will help feed the people of developing nations, such as those in Africa where agricultural conditions are indeed harsh. Opponents fear that the impact of genetic modification has not been adequately studied and thus such crops pose a potential threat to human health and the environment. A similar debate is raging among those who support and oppose the development of GM fish. While some suggest that the development of GM fish might reduce the pressure on the marine environment, others fear that GM fish might put wild stocks at risk. Indeed, one of many controversies in the fisheries debate is whether the risks of genetically engineered fish outweigh the benefits.

Biotechnology researchers are working to develop seafood and aquatic plants that grow faster, resist disease, and tolerate cold water. One goal is to come up with farmed fish that convert feed more efficiently and that produce less marine waste. Aqua Bounty Technologies is seeking approval to sell its AquAdvantage salmon, which has been genetically modified to grow all year, not just in the summer, when salmon normally develop. These salmon will also reach marketable size twice as fast, thus saving fish farmers money on feed. Moreover, salmon that mature more quickly will also release less waste into the marine environment. Roger Berkowitz, president and CEO of Legal Sea Foods, a restaurant chain, claims that if GM fish were deemed safe, had the same nutritional benefits, and good flavor, he would consider putting it on the menu. "Anything that takes the pressure off wild stocks and has the potential to feed more people is good," he claims.

Opponents worry about the impact of GM fish on the integrity of wild stocks. They fear that GM fish might breed with wild stocks and deplete the gene pool. Moreover, if GM fish were to escape from farms in areas where they have no natural predators, they might compete with or prey on other wild fish species. Environmental policy professor and member of the U.S. Commission on Ocean Policy Andrew Rosenberg asks, "What happens if they escape? . . . Producers may say the odds are 95 percent against escape, but other things work 95 percent of the time too, like condoms, and that's not always good enough." Other critics question whether genetic modifications are that much better than traditional breeding techniques. Fish farming already cultivates fish much faster than land plants and animals. "With conventional animal breeding technologies we can get phenomenal gains in growth and other favorable characteristics," claims University of Rhode Island fisheries and aquaculture professor Barry Costa-Pierce. "I doubt there's a big market for GM fish in North America, so why go down a path of conflict and controversy that could undercut markets for conventional products?" he reasons. Indeed, California, Oregon, and Washington have banned raising GM fish in state waters.

Analysts on both sides of the controversy continue to debate the benefits and risks of genetically engineered fish and their potential impact on the world's oceans. The authors in the following chapter present their views on how best to promote sustainable fishing in the world's oceans.

> "Because wild harvests can no longer
> keep up with growing demand, in-
> creases in the seafood supply will come
> from aquaculture."

Aquaculture Will Fill the Gap in the Seafood Supply

William T. Hogarth

Aquaculture, the farming of fish and other aquatic organisms, will help meet America's growing demand for seafood, argues William T. Hogarth in the following viewpoint. Despite improved management practices, America's wild fisheries have been unable to meet the growing demand, he contends. Indeed, Hogarth claims, the United States imports a significant portion of the seafood it consumes. Aquaculture will increase domestic seafood production, improve seafood safety, and create jobs in America's coastal communities, he asserts. Hogarth was, at the time of this writing, director of the National Marine Fisheries Service, part of the National Oceanic and Atmospheric Administration.

As you read, consider the following questions:

1. According to Hogarth, what percentage of the seafood consumed worldwide is farmed?

William T. Hogarth, "Offshore Aquaculture Fills the Supply Gap," *SeaFood Business*, September 2007. Copyright © 2007 SeaFood Business. Reproduced by permission.

2. What percentage of the seafood consumed in the United States is imported, in the author's view?

3. In Hogarth's opinion, what will be the ripple effect of environmentally sound aquaculture expansion?

When it comes to seafood production, the United States is at a crossroads. Study after study confirms the health benefits of eating seafood, and consumers in America and abroad have gotten the message. Meanwhile, wild catch levels worldwide have remained relatively stable over the last 20 years. Because wild harvests can no longer keep up with growing demand, increases in the seafood supply will come from aquaculture.

We've done a good job managing America's marine resources, but even the best-managed wild fisheries can't meet the growing demand for seafood. Aquaculture must fill the gap—the only question is, where will it come from?

Aquaculture is a $70 billion annual enterprise worldwide; almost half of the seafood consumed is farmed. However, U.S. aquaculture accounts for just 1.5 percent of the global aquaculture production. Experts say we'll need another 40 million tons of seafood annually by 2030 to meet current consumption rates.

Expanding Aquaculture

In this large and growing market, the United States remains a net importer of seafood—more than 80 percent of the seafood consumed in the United States is imported, of which 40 percent is farmed. Marine aquaculture therefore presents tremendous opportunities for the United States.

Enactment of the National Offshore Aquaculture Act of 2007 will allow the United States to become more self-sufficient in the production of healthy seafood by growing more at home.

By laying the foundation for aquaculture expansion, the bill will help create jobs in coastal communities and help re-

The Consumption of Farmed Seafood Is Rising

Aquaculture accounted for nearly half of all seafood eaten worldwide in 2005, compared with slightly more than a third in 2000. During the same period, total consumption of seafood (both farmed and wild) rose to nearly 100 million tons.

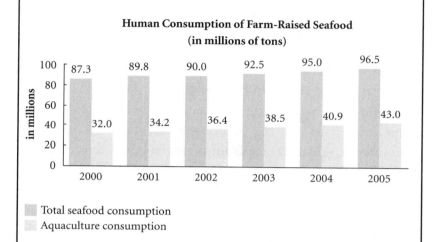

Human Consumption of Farm-Raised Seafood
(in millions of tons)

Total seafood consumption values: 87.3 (2000), 89.8 (2001), 90.0 (2002), 92.5 (2003), 95.0 (2004), 96.5 (2005)

Aquaculture consumption values: 32.0 (2000), 34.2 (2001), 36.4 (2002), 38.5 (2003), 40.9 (2004), 43.0 (2005)

■ Total seafood consumption
■ Aquaculture consumption

TAKEN FROM: "The State of World Fisheries and Aquaculture 2006," Food and Agriculture Organization of the United Nations, 2007.

duce our $8 billion seafood trade deficit. The United States must develop aquaculture as a complement to commercial fishing or it will be forced to import increasing amounts of farm-raised seafood.

Food safety is another issue. U.S. consumers want to know that their seafood was produced in a safe and sustainable way, and many turn to local products when given a choice. Producing seafood locally allows us to test and develop new technologies, equipment and alternative feeds. This makes us more competitive in the global market and allows us to lead by example—our sustainable production will encourage our trading partners to adopt best management practices, thereby improving the quality of all seafood reaching U.S. consumers.

An Economic Boon

For some time, many coastal communities have suffered from overcapitalization and limited harvests in the commercial fishing industry. With a robust domestic aquaculture industry, fishing boats could also service aquaculture operations, and seafood-industry infrastructure could process and distribute both cultured and wild seafood products.

Domestic aquaculture could provide a steady source of product and, in some locations, prevent processing facilities from closing down due to insufficient wild harvests.

Preliminary production estimates indicate that domestic aquaculture production of all species (both marine and freshwater) could increase from about 500,000 tons today to more than 1.5 million tons per year by 2025. The additional production could include 760,000 tons of seafood from finfish aquaculture and 245,000 tons from mollusk production.

In addition to creating new job opportunities at hatcheries and grow-out facilities, environmentally sound aquaculture expansion will have a ripple effect on other aspects of the economy since aquaculture relies on other producers and manufacturers for goods and services, including soybean and grain producers; equipment and technology providers; cold storage, transport, marketing and foodservice providers; and veterinarians. In turn, these activities will strengthen the coastal communities in which the businesses operate and provide healthy seafood to consumers.

Successes to date of aquaculture-related businesses demonstrate direct economic benefits from an increase in domestic aquaculture production, including offshore aquaculture. More and more communities and fishermen are recognizing that environmentally sound aquaculture can present development opportunities for areas hit hard by job losses, natural disasters and other challenges. As interest grows, these communities are beginning to integrate aquaculture into their economies. Stock enhancement of commercial and recreational fisheries adds to the economic benefits accruing from U.S. investment in marine aquaculture.

Striking a Balance

The bill strikes the proper balance between aquaculture development and environmental protection and will allow for timely permit decisions and adaptive management approaches. It also includes provisions for R&D [research and development] to support all types of marine aquaculture, not just offshore technologies.

Marine aquaculture has the potential to contribute greatly to our seafood supply and to the economy. But this potential will be realized only if we can provide the regulatory certainty for businesses to make sound investment decisions. The National Offshore Aquaculture Act of 2007 will give NOAA [National Oceanic and Atmospheric Administration] the authority it needs to provide that regulatory certainty.

> "The way [aquaculture] is being done in many parts of the world is not sustainable and comes with high environmental costs."

Aquaculture Practices Are Inefficient

Ken Hinman

Current aquaculture practices are inefficient and not sustainable, claims Ken Hinman in the following viewpoint. In fact, he maintains, most of today's fisheries no longer provide seafood for the American dinner table. Instead, Hinman asserts, they raise fish such as menhaden, sardines, and mackerel to provide feed for livestock and for other farmed fish. Feeding carnivorous farm-raised salmon and tuna depletes more fish than it produces for food, making current aquaculture practices inefficient and unsustainable, he reasons. Hinman is president of the National Coalition for Marine Conservation.

As you read, consider the following questions:

1. In what way is the U.S. Department of Commerce's claim that Americans ate 16.5 pounds of seafood per person in 2006 deceiving, according to Hinman?

Ken Hinman, "Catch All You Want, We'll Make More," *Marine Bulletin*, Fall 2007. Copyright © 1999–2008 National Coalition for Marine Conservation. Reproduced by permission.

2. How many pounds of forage fish does it take to feed salmon and tuna, in the author's opinion?

3. How, in the view of Hinman, should the United States proceed with aquaculture?

A mericans ate an average of 16 1/2 pounds of seafood per person in 2006, according to the U.S. Department of Commerce. What would seem to be good news for the fishing industry is tempered by the fact that 83 percent of the fresh, frozen or canned fish and shellfish we consume are imported from overseas. Forty percent of that comes from fish farms.

Questioning the Claims

The [George W. Bush] Administration is using these figures to bolster support for legislation to promote a big-time U.S. off-shore aquaculture industry to close the trade deficit by making the country more seafood self-sufficient.

The National Marine Fisheries Service, a branch of the Commerce Department, claims aquaculture will take pressure off wild stocks as seafood demand in the U.S. is expected to exceed supply—stocks are already strained beyond capacity—by 4 million metric tons by 2025.

But will farming take the pressure off? Can we really get more fish out of the ocean without taking more fish?

Only two of the five largest capture fisheries produce seafood directly for our dinner table, according to the Woods Hole Oceanographic Institution. The other three "reduce" fish such as menhaden, sardine and mackerel to fish meal and oil for agriculture and aquaculture feeds. So the 16 lbs per person is deceiving. It's actually a lot more than that—up to 4 times, by one estimate—when you factor in the animals nourished on fish feed—chickens, pigs and, yes, farmed fish.

An Ineffective Strategy

With the exploding global growth of marine aquaculture, including penning or ranching carnivorous fish like salmon and

"Thanks to a little genetic engineering, we can merchandise these fish right on the farm."

tuna, we're likely to see a sizeable increase in the amount of fish removed from the ocean to feed them.

Diverting fish to the table through farming is an inefficient way to use protein from the sea. More than 3 pounds of forage fish are needed to raise a pound of salmon. For a pound of tuna, it takes 20 pounds. Stocks of key forage fish are not well managed around the world and cannot handle the increased fishing pressure. Even in the U.S., target populations are set to sustain the fisheries, not predators.

As for whether aquaculture will take pressure off the stocks of the fish being farmed, that hasn't happened with salmon, because wild-caught fish are more valuable. And in the Mediterranean [Med], where farming bluefin tuna is big business, the result has been vastly increased captures of wild tuna to "grow" in the pens, without a commensurate drop-off in the established market fisheries. Farming adds an estimated 25,000 tons a year to what's already being taken from the Med. Annual catches are now over 50,000 tons, in a fishery that scientists say shouldn't take more than 15,000.

This is not to say there isn't room for aquaculture in the sea. But the way it's being done in many parts of the world is not sustainable and comes with high environmental costs. The U.S. must proceed slowly and carefully to protect our wild fisheries, commercial and recreational, and the food base they depend on.

"Bottom trawling has become the greatest threat to deep sea ecology."

Banning Bottom Trawling Would Protect Deep Sea Ecology

Joshua Reichert

According to Joshua Reichert in the following viewpoint, marine scientists generally agree that deep sea bottom trawling is an unnecessary, destructive fishing practice. Bottom trawling destroys the fragile deep sea habitat on which many species depend, he claims. Moreover, Reichert maintains, many of the life forms destroyed take centuries to recover. Indeed, the threat posed by bottom trawling far outweighs any negligible benefits, he asserts. Nevertheless, Reichert argues, destructive bottom trawling remains largely unregulated. Reichert directs the environment program of the Pew Charitable Trusts, some of the nation's most influential conservation policy groups.

As you read, consider the following questions:

1. What part of the world's oceans does Reichert claim are the patrimony of all humanity?

2. Why, in the author's view, are the areas destroyed by unregulated bottom trawling of inestimable biological and ecological value?

3. According to Reichert, which nations favor and which oppose bottom trawling?

In weighty discussions that have been quietly taking place at the United Nations, one topic has received little public attention: a proposal to halt unregulated bottom trawling on the high seas. The world's oceans that lie beyond 200 miles from shore are not under the jurisdiction of any single country but are considered to be the patrimony of all humanity. The proposal has huge global significance. If such a moratorium were enacted it would constitute the single most sweeping act of habitat protection in human history, covering an estimated 67 million square miles of ocean, an area larger than all of the world's continents combined.

Destructive Fishing Gear

Considered by many marine scientists to be the most destructive fishing gear in the world's oceans, deep sea bottom trawls consist of nets the size of football fields that can reach down more than a mile beneath the water's surface. Weighted down by massive steel doors and often attached to heavy rollers, these nets can weigh five tons or more. When dragged across the ocean floor, they frequently crush everything in their path.

Not only do these trawls break up the delicate structure of seamounts and deep-water corals that provide critical habitat to countless species of fish and other marine life, they also contribute to the serial depletion of deep sea fisheries. Moreover, because these corals, fish and other life forms are very slow growing, they can take centuries or more to recover, if they do at all.

Many of the areas destroyed by unregulated bottom trawls are of inestimable biological and ecological value. Scientists

Threat to Deep Sea Ecology

Every year an area of the ocean floor twice the size of the United States is decimated by trawling, a fishing practice whereby powerful vessels drag enormous nets on heavy metal frames. Modern technology has enabled trawlers to operate in the deep sea where bottom trawling has become the greatest threat to deep sea ecology. Covering more than half of the earth's surface, the deep sea supports millions of terrestrial and aquatic organisms. As a result, it assists breeding and feeding of organisms in shallower waters that support marine fisheries worldwide. The deep sea also contains biologically rich submerged mountains called seamounts that serve as an oasis of biological productivity in the open ocean. Bottom trawling scrapes these seamounts and other deep sea structures clean, easily devastating entire ecosystems.

Anna Vinson,
Georgetown International Environmental Law Review,
Winter 2006.

calculate that the deep sea contains millions of species, along with entire ecosystems that are found nowhere else on earth. Many of these have yet to be identified by science, much less assessed for their potential value to people in the form of medicines and other products that can help enhance human life.

In 2001, the last year for which good data are available, there were only an estimated 200-to-300 vessels involved in high seas bottom trawling, a tiny fraction of the estimated three million fishing vessels in operation worldwide. The world's bottom-trawl fleet netted less than one half of one percent of the estimated value of the global catch of marine fish.

Negligible Economic Value

By almost any standard, the economic value of this type of fishing is negligible, even more so when you consider that it is being propped up by subsidies. Indeed, a recent study by Rashid Sumaila, an economist at the University of British Columbia in Vancouver, estimates that if you remove the subsidies that are given each year to the high seas bottom-trawl fleet, these vessels would be operating at a loss and would be unable to continue fishing.

When the social and economic benefits of unregulated high seas bottom trawling are contrasted to the vast damage it does to some of the most vulnerable and fragile marine habitats on earth, it is simply foolish for the global community to let it continue. . . .

Numerous countries including Australia, New Zealand, Brazil, the United States and many northern European nations are advocating a halt to this practice. However, a handful of other countries like Japan, Canada, Iceland and Spain are working to block UN action.

Allowing this kind of unregulated destructive fishing to continue is not in the long-term interest of humanity. Ultimately, we have far more to gain from protecting the places being destroyed by these trawls than we do from allowing them to be irresponsibly fished.

This is a problem we can solve, and solve quickly. There are relatively few boats and people involved, and not much vested economic interest that would be compromised by halting the fishing. There is an opportunity to do this now, before a lot more damage is done. Hopefully the world's nations, those who fish and those who don't, will not let it slip by.

> *"Unless fishing . . . shifts back to primitive and inefficient technologies, harvesting the fish and shellfish that are found on or near the bottom is going to have an impact on that bottom."*

Expecting Fishing Technologies to Have No Ecological Impact Is Unreasonable

Nils Stolpe

Fishing technologies, like agricultural technologies, will always have an impact on the environment, maintains Nils Stolpe in the following viewpoint. Nevertheless, he claims, many environmentalists unfairly insist that fishing technologies should have no impact on the marine environment. Unless fishermen revert to primitive fishing technologies, Stolpe argues, harvesting bottom fish to feed the world's growing population will necessarily have some impact. Even so, he asserts, fishermen are constantly working to minimize the impact of harvesting fish. Stolpe is a long-time consultant to the commercial fishing industry.

As you read, consider the following questions:

1. According to the Food and Agriculture Organization, as cited by the author, how much of the world's land area is devoted to grazing or growing livestock for feed?

2. In Stolpe's view, what is memorialized in "America the Beautiful"?

3. What is used to create artificial reefs, and seems to contradict the claims of environmentalists, in the author's opinion?

The United Nations Food and Agriculture Organization [FAO] reported that in 2002 the world production of pork was 95 million tons, poultry was 72 million tons, beef was 60 million tons and goat was 11 million tons.

The Impact of Agriculture

You don't have to be an agricultural expert to know that neither a cornfield nor a heavily grazed pasture bears much resemblance to virgin grassland or forest. If you've driven across North America, you know that you can go for miles without seeing much more than wheat, corn or soybean fields. And if you've flown cross-country and spent any time looking out the window, for much of the flight the most noticeable feature has to be a seemingly endless progression of cultivated fields.

Of course, this agricultural development isn't limited to North America. According to the FAO, about a fourth of the world's land area is devoted to either growing livestock feed or for grazing. Humankind's insatiable appetite for calories has drastically altered the terrestrial ecosystems of all but one of our continents.

No one is insisting that we should be producing all of this livestock, using all of this land, without any impact on the environment.

Duping the Public

Opponents of bottom trawling have done a good job of duping the public and, unfortunately, many fishery scientists, into believing bottom trawling is the same as bulldozing the sea bottom. . . .

There is no similarity between bulldozers and trawl nets. . . . A bottom trawl . . . does not dig like a bulldozer.

Gary Loverich, National Fisherman, *January 2007.*

The production of fish and seafood surpasses that of any other animal protein. In 2002 it was just over 100 million metric tons (a level that it's hovered around for years).

Yet, while accepting a world that has been radically altered by agriculture, some so-called environmentalists insist that in the act of producing a greater tonnage of protein than cattle ranchers or poultry farmers do, commercial fishermen should be prevented from having any effect on the ocean environment. They actually preach that, for whatever reasons happen to be in vogue at the moment, the oceans should remain pristine and free from fishing's impacts.

According to them, fishing gear and techniques that have any impact on the ocean ecosystem are unacceptable. Going back almost a decade, they were bolstering their arguments by comparing the size of nets to Boeing 747 airliners. Then they segued into gear "bulldozing" or "clear cutting" areas of ocean bottom the size of continental land masses. Most recently, it has been the destruction of "luxurious forests" of deep water corals, supposed critical areas that few if any in the environmental community had paid any attention to up until the time when fishing gear was implicated in their supposed destruction.

It's perfectly obvious that we aren't going to have any agricultural production without affecting the terrestrial environment; in fact, it's memorialized in "America the Beautiful," with fruited plains and amber waves. No agricultural impacts equal no agriculture.

So, should we be expected to fish—at least at any meaningful level of production—while having no impacts on the ocean environment? Any rational analysis would suggest we shouldn't, but since when have the anti-fishing forces been interested in rationality?

Harvesting Causes Change

The very act of harvesting fish causes change. While a stock can be fished sustainably with 20 percent or 30 percent or more of the biomass being removed every year, that removal will have an impact.

Then there are the impacts of fishing gear. Dragging a net or a dredge across it is definitely going to alter the bottom, and anything that alters the bottom is anathema to these "environmentalists." Or is it? When creating artificial reefs, natural bottom is covered with thousands of tons of surplus weaponry, decommissioned ships, construction rubble and obsolete subway cars. When was the last time one of the conspicuously anti–commercial fishing organizations demanded that the natural bottom be protected from burial by megatons of societal refuse? (I have to acknowledge here Clean Ocean Action's valiant attempts to keep the waters in the New York Bight from being used as a convenient junk yard.) It seems like some alterations are OK.

It should go without saying, but the bottom impacts fishing gear as much as the gear impacts the bottom. More "wear and tear" on the bottom means more wear and tear on the gear, and that means higher operating costs. Gear researchers and fishermen have been working on nets and dredges that

145

fish "lighter" for years, but today's [2005] $3-a-gallon fuel makes improvements in this area imperative.

Unless fishing effort shifts back to primitive and inefficient technologies, harvesting the fish and shellfish that are found on or near the bottom is going to have an impact on that bottom. We can, and we are, working constantly to reduce that impact, but we're not going to get away from it without regressing to hand harvesting methods in use centuries ago. With the world's population at seven billion and rising, this isn't going to happen. Isn't it time we started working toward a public policy that accepts this while still protecting the areas that need to be protected?

"The increase in fish stocks and habitat recovery within marine reserves has been well documented."

Marine Reserves Will Preserve Dwindling Fish Stocks

Bijal P. Trivedi

In the following viewpoint, Bijal P. Trivedi claims that a network of marine reserves would reduce the impact of overfishing. While the increase in fish stock and habit recovery within marine reserves has been documented, now studies are finding that marine reserves influence fish stocks in surrounding fisheries as well. Although marine reserves benefit fish and their delicate habitats, there are still waves of resistance from fishermen who believe marine reserves could end their way of life. However, the author believes, once fishermen see the benefits, most will drop their arguments. Bijal P. Trivedi writes for National Geographic.

As you read, consider the following questions:

1. According to Trivedi, what percentage of fishing grounds did St. Lucia set aside for a marine reserve?

2. Why is it better to have fewer big fish than many small fish, according to the expert cited by the author?

Bijal P. Trivedi, "Marine Reserves Found to Boost Nearby Fishing Grounds," *National Geographic*, December 4, 2001. Copyright © 2001 National Geographic Society. Reproduced by permission.

3. Why are the fishing industries on the verge of disaster, according to the scientist cited by Trivedi?

In 1995, the people of the Caribbean island of St. Lucia had grown alarmed by local fish harvests that were so paltry they could barely sustain their families. In a desperate effort to revive the overexploited reefs, they created a marine reserve and banned fishing in 35 percent of their fishing grounds.

Today, the people are reaping the rewards of their gamble as they watch their catch sizes double and triple in waters neighboring the sanctuary.

"When we went there in 1994, the fishermen could spend several hours rowing to a fishing spot—a whole day on the water—and catch barely a handful of fish," said marine conservation biologist Callum Roberts of the University of York in the United Kingdom. "It was hardly worth the effort."

Roberts and his colleagues studied the marine reserve bordering St. Lucia and one in Florida to determine the impacts on neighboring fisheries. The results showed that the creation of marine sanctuaries significantly increased both fish yields and the size of fish in surrounding areas.

The St. Lucians' decision to set aside 35 percent of their fishing grounds—creating the Soufrière Marine Management Area—was locally contentious. But although the first two years were particularly tough, local fishermen are now reaping the benefits of the reserve. With the fisheries replenished, they are enjoying the spillover, with much higher harvests than before the reserve was established even though there are fewer regions to fish, said Roberts.

The increase in fish stocks and habitat recovery within marine reserves has been well documented. Until now, however, the impact of such reserves on surrounding fisheries had not been evaluated. Roberts believes his study, which is published in the November 30 [2001] issue of the journal *Science*, provides this link.

Role of Marine Reserves

Marine reserves and conventional tools have many common goals but reserves should be integrated into the fishery management toolkit because they can achieve things that other tools cannot. There is no legal means of fishing in a marine reserve, so there is no lawful way of undermining the protection they afford to species and habitats. There is no surer way of integrating ecosystem-level concerns into fishery management than protecting entire, intact ecosystems. Short of changing human nature, existing management tools offer few options for mitigating risky decision-making where the final choices on catches lie with politicians or industry representatives. . . . Marine reserves can complement other fishery management tools in order to deliver sustainable fisheries and meet conservation objectives.

Callum M. Roberts, Julie P. Hawkins, and Fiona R. Gell,
Philosophical Transactions of the Royal Society, *2005.*

Record Catches

Roberts and his team also studied a marine reserve in Merritt Island National Wildlife Refuge at Cape Canaveral, Florida, which is one of the oldest marine sanctuaries in the United States.

Ironically, the reserve, where fishing and public access have been prohibited since 1962, was established to protect rockets, not fish. Because it is near Kennedy Space Center, access was prohibited for security reasons. The area off limits included estuarine habitats that were particularly rich breeding grounds for several game-fish species—black drum, red drum, spotted sea trout, and common snook.

This area has been undisturbed for nearly 40 years, which gives scientists the opportunity to study how local marine resources have been affected.

One of the biggest payoffs, the scientists found, is that species that grow slowly can reach their full potential. The black drum, whose lifespan may reach 70 years, can grow up to 100 pounds (45 kilograms).

It's better to have fewer big fish rather than many small fish, said Roberts, because big fish produce more eggs. "A single 20-pound grouper can produce more eggs than 93 one-pound groupers," he explained.

The International Game Fish Association, which registers record-breaking fish catches from around the world, has found that the waters within 62 miles (100 kilometers) of the Merritt Island Refuge yield more record-breaking big fish than all other Florida waters combined.

Multiple Benefits

Marine reserves benefit not only fish but also delicate habitats.

Trawling—essentially plowing the ocean bottom to harvest scallops and shrimp—is a particularly destructive method of fishing. "[Marine scientist] Sylvia Earle compared trawling to cutting a forest to catch squirrels," said Roberts.

Marine reserves protect ocean bottom, enabling the undersea environment to recover. Closing off a portion of northeastern fisheries in Georges Bank off the coast of New England to ground fishing has led to the best scallop season in a decade, said Roberts. And flounder, which had been severely overfished, is on the road to recovery as a result of putting some fishing areas off limits.

"Marine reserves are like money in the bank for fishers," said Fiona Gell, also of the University of York and a co-author of the study. "If you want to keep a population going, you have to provide safe havens where fish and their habitats can flourish."

Currently in California, legislators are weighing the benefits of the Marine Life Protection Act, which would establish a string of no-fishing zones along the California coastline. But as in St. Lucia, setting up these reserves is a politically charged and highly emotional issue.

The fishing industries are on the verge of disaster, said fisheries biologist Alec MacCall of the Southwest Fisheries Science Center in Santa Cruz, California. "Fishing quotas have been so low that fishermen are barely able to make a living."

Wave of Resistance

Recognition that habitat loss and overfishing cannot sustain existing fishing levels led to the U.S. 1996 Sustainable Fisheries Act, which limits the size of catches and by-catches, thereby allowing depleted fish stocks to rebound. But fishermen already hurting from low catches and quotas are concerned that creating reserves will deliver a final crippling blow to their livelihood.

Most fishermen agree with the concept of marine reserves, but want them implemented in someone else's area, said Mac-Call.

"Fishing is almost the last frontier—people can fish just about anywhere and anyhow, but creating marine reserves is like creating fences in the ocean," he said. "It ends a way of life, it ends an era."

MacCall believes that marine reserves are a long-term investment, without which fisheries are likely to experience "boom-bust cycles." He is particularly interested in the effect of such reserves on marine habitats. Nonetheless, he thinks conservationists are overselling the merit of the approach.

"It's a great idea but should not be oversold as a panacea to severely depleted fish stocks," said MacCall. Migratory fish, such as albacore and bluefin tuna, will not be well protected by reserves, for example. On the other hand, orange roughy—

which grow slowly, can live up to 150 years, and tend to settle in one location—may be well served by sanctuaries.

"The ocean is a complicated place and you can't predict the population benefits of creating these reserves," said McCall. "It's the sort of thing you just do, and then you wait and see."

"*[Advocating] blanket no-fishing zones . . . removes the incentive for a shift to the use of more selective, sustainable and habitat-friendly fishing methods.*"

Marine Reserves Will Not Stop Destructive Fishing Practices

National Coalition for Marine Conservation

Marine reserves that prohibit fishing will not prevent destructive fishing practices, maintains the National Coalition for Marine Conservation (NCMC) in the following viewpoint. Just as designating wilderness areas has done nothing to prevent uncontrolled human development on land, marine reserves do nothing to reduce the destruction of marine habitats, NCMC claims. Marine conservation efforts should promote sustainable practices in all marine environments, not just specific areas, NCMC reasons. NCMC is an advocacy group dedicated to protecting marine fish and the marine environment.

As you read, consider the following questions:

1. In what has the system of National Parks and Wilderness Areas resulted, according to NCMC?

2. What type of process does NCMC recommend for the development of a Marine Protected Area?

3. What went wrong in California waters, in the opinion of NCMC?

The use of Marine Protected Areas [MPAs] also called marine reserves, as a fishery management tool is a hot topic of discussion amongst the marine conservation community. Overfishing, and the continued failure to satisfactorily control this widespread problem, is driving support for the use of reserves, including areas where all fishing is prohibited. Unfortunately, the ongoing debate has polarized the issue, holding up a constructive process for examining the utility of MPAs.

The MPA concept embraces a range of management options, many of which are already in use. It is wrong to perceive it as simply establishing areas where all forms of fishing are prohibited. The National Coalition for Marine Conservation (NCMC) believes the time is ripe for a more focused discussion to define the purpose of MPAs and to describe a process for developing and establishing areas of special protection in the ocean.

NCMC believes reserves should be considered as a solution to a specific problem or to achieve a specific purpose and designed with that goal in mind. We are opposed to the use of blanket no-take zones, under the belief that activities should not be restricted unless they are demonstrably causing a specific conservation problem. No-fishing zones, and NCMC's solution to developing fair and effective MPAs, are discussed in detail below.

No Panacea

First, a cautionary note. Proponents of MPAs like to point to our country's National Parks and Wilderness Areas and argue that similar kinds of "preserves" are needed in the ocean. The underlying assumption is that the parks and wilderness system has been an effective way to conserve ecosystems on land. Before we seek to replicate this type of "zoning" at sea, however, we must ask ourselves if we really want management of our oceans to mirror a system wherein we give extraordinary protection to a few prescribed areas while allowing helter-skelter land-use beyond their borders.

Vast areas of land in this country are overrun with development, from sprawling metropolitan and suburban areas to poorly managed grazing, mining, and forestry practices in more rural areas. The system of National Parks and Wilderness Areas has only resulted in isolated pockets of nearly pristine wilderness surrounded by relatively uncontrolled human development. Underdeveloped areas outside this system remain vulnerable to potential misuse or abuse. NCMC firmly believes that such a system will be inadequate to maintain and propagate our vast marine ecosystems.

What we should be striving for is a more conservative approach to managing the oceans as a whole. Methods of harvesting our ocean resources that are selective and sustainable should be encouraged and promoted, while non-selective fishing methods and destructive fishing gears should be phased out. It is these unsustainable fishing practices that are largely responsible for the overfishing and other problems that are driving support for the use of reserves in the first place. It is these practices that should be restricted, not fishing per se.

Indeed, while it is true that most human activities are excluded from wilderness areas, including all commercial enterprises and development, it is only those that threaten their integrity. The Bob Marshall Wilderness in western Montana, for example, is the largest and arguably the wildest—grizzly bears thrive there—in the lower 48 states. Fishing, hunting, camping, hiking and other recreational activities are not only allowed, they are encouraged—within strictly defined rules, of couse.

The wilderness concept on land, therefore, is not a closed-door policy. Even our most sheltered wilderness areas allow some human activities, including certain kinds of fishing, because they are entirely compatible with the wilderness experience. Why should ocean wilderness be any different?

Promoting Sustainable Fishing

The problem with advocating blanket no-fishing zones as a solution to our fishery management ills is that it presumes that all fishing methods and gears are equally harmful. It removes the incentive for a shift to the use of more selective, sustainable and habitat-friendly fishing methods throughout our oceans.

NCMC's suggested process for designating areas for special protection advances this shift to sustainability. By identifying specific conservation problems and their direct causes, destructive activities can be excluded from areas where they are causing problems. At the same time, fishermen who use selective and low-impact fishing gears and methods can be rewarded with continued access to fishing grounds. Not only will this process result in reserves that are managed fairly and equitably, it will create incentives to move away from destructive fishing practices, thus benefiting the entire ocean and not just isolated areas.

Having said that, no-fishing marine reserves may be necessary under certain circumstances. If it can be demonstrated that all fishing activities are causing a conservation problem in a specific area, then it is justifiable to exclude these activities. NCMC could also support fully protected reserves, select in number and relatively discrete in size, for research purposes to help define a benchmark marine ecosystem useful for comparing and evaluating human impacts in ecologically sensitive areas.

Marine Reserve Drawbacks

Opponents of marine reserves commonly cite four major drawbacks:

1. Marine reserves are difficult to properly design and site;

2. Marine reserves displace fishermen;

3. Marine reserves offer incomplete protection; and

4. Marine reserves may be expensive to enforce.

National Fisheries Conservation Center, undated.

A Goal-Oriented Approach

Development of any MPA should be a bottom-up process beginning with the identification of sensitive areas where species or critical habitats need protection and ending with the specific regulation necessary to provide that protection, not vice-versa. Up to this point, discussion of MPAs has tended toward a top-down approach. In other words, the process begins with the idea that a fully protected reserve might benefit many species and habitats that have been adversely impacted by overfishing and moves from there. Using such a top-down approach may result in unfairly restricting access to user groups who are not responsible for causing or contributing to any specific conservation problem.

Whether we are talking about commercial or recreational fishing activities, NCMC prefers that activities be restricted or prohibited strictly on the basis of their causing a demonstrable problem. Identifying problem activities should be the governing criteria for prohibitions in an MPA. In the same way, we do not believe that all user groups should be excluded from an MPA simply to achieve "fairness." The only truly fair MPA is where problem activities are restricted and benign activities are not.

Reserves Done Right

Several positive examples already exist of this bottom-up approach to developing reserves. One is the set of seasonal area closures to longline fishing in the Atlantic to reduce bycatch of overfished pelagic species. In this case, fishery managers began with a specific conservation problem—large numbers of juvenile swordfish, marlin and sharks being killed on indiscriminate longline gear in areas where they concentrate—and ended with a type of reserve where the activity causing the problem (longlining) is prohibited when and where the problem is most acute.

Another example is the Dry Tortugas reserve in the Florida Keys. The confluence of currents in this area where the Gulf of Mexico meets the Straits of Florida has produced a highly unique ecosystem with abundant marine life. A limited part of this area is designated as no-take, and lesser restrictions apply in adjacent sections. The uniqueness of this relatively small area and the research benefits stemming from it being reserved warranted the restrictions.

Reserves Done Wrong

The most notorious example of the reserve movement gone awry is in California waters. The state legislature passed the Marine Life Protection Act (MLPA), which mandated that a certain percentage of waters be closed to various types of fishing. This is a top-down approach, where managers started not with the goal of solving a specific conservation problem, but with the specious goal of closing down large swaths of ocean to fishing, without sufficient justification or rationale. The result is that commercial and recreational fishermen have lost access to popular fishing grounds, with little consideration given to whether their activities were damaging or that specific problems would be solved as a result of sweeping closures. California's process of developing reserves under the MLPA was fundamentally flawed; backward, unfair, arbitrary and ultimately counterproductive to obtaining improved conservation. Yet the closures were recently put into effect.

In another case, the Gulf of Mexico Fishery Management Council proposed a closed area to protect spawning aggregations of gag grouper. The Council originally recommended closing the known spawning area to all types of fishing. But the specific problem was that gag grouper were being caught during the spawn by bottom-fishermen; surface fishing for marlin, tuna, dolphin and mackerel occurred in the area without a remote chance of hooking grouper. Excluding these surface fisheries would have resulted in no additional protection to gag grouper and was thus unjustifiable. The Council lost a legal challenge to its arbitrary closure and now the spawning area is closed to bottom fishing only. . . .

In conclusion, we believe Marine Protected Areas can serve as a useful tool for effective marine fisheries conservation if properly and judiciously employed. We believe it is important to define and adhere to a specified development process for any future MPAs. . . . In the end, we will be fostering a more conservative approach to managing the oceans as a whole, encouraging the use of selective and sustainable fishing gears and practices while eliminating the use of those that aren't.

> "The result [of fishing quotas] is that
> fisheries are being sustainably harvested
> and the export value of their products
> went up 400 percent."

Individual Fishing Quotas Benefit U.S. Fisheries

Ronald Bailey

Individual Fishing Quotas (IFQs), the permission to catch a percentage of the total allowable catch, are an effective way to manage U.S. fisheries, claims libertarian writer Ronald Bailey in the following viewpoint. Not only do IFQs prevent overfishing, the author argues, IFQs improve fishing safety and allow fishing in good weather conditions. In addition, IFQs reduce the cheating that accompanies strict regulations, the author maintains. Ronald Bailey is a science correspondent at Reason *magazine.*

As you read, consider the following questions:

1. What does the author claim is the chief problem with U.S. fisheries?
2. Is a season longer or shorter under IFQs, according to Bailey?

3. Of worldwide fisheries revenues of $100 billion, what
   does Bailey say is the annual loss?

The pitiful state of America's ocean fisheries provokes pe-
rennial handwringing. In its July 31st [2006] issue, *The
New Yorker* profiled historical ecologist, fisher and MacArthur
genius Ted Ames. Mining the memories of old fishers and historical documents, Ames has rediscovered the former spawning and feeding grounds of ghost cod populations in the Gulf
of Maine that were destroyed by overfishing. The hope is that
that knowledge will aid in some day restoring them. The profile notes that with modern fishing methods "[e]ntire populations of fish can be erased." In fact, New England's once vast
cod fishery is all but gone today.

Current State of U.S. Fisheries

Nowhere in *The New Yorker* profile does the concept of the
tragedy of the commons appear. This is an odd omission because it is the explanation for why so many of the world's
fisheries, including New England's, are being devastated. The
tragedy of the commons occurs when resources can be exploited by anyone. In open access fisheries, no fisher has an
incentive to leave any fish behind to breed because he knows
that the next fisher that comes along will simply take whatever
fish he leaves and sell it. It's a race to the bottom with both
fish and fishers losing out. This race to the bottom has all but
destroyed New England's famous cod, haddock and flounder
fisheries.

The New Yorker profile notes that Maine's lobster fisheries
remain healthy and productive, but attributes that success
mostly to "stringent practices" such as state-mandated size
limits. The profile does mention in passing: "Lobstermen in-
formally divide the ocean among the towns and precincts
whose shores it borders. A lobsterman from one town who
drops his traps in another town's waters can expect to find his
strings cut and his traps disappeared." In other words, Maine

"harbor gangs" avoid the tragedy of commons in their fisheries because they treat their local lobster fisheries as their private communal property and exclude outsiders. In other words, property rights, even informal property rights, can help restore and protect fisheries.

In early June [2006], the Philanthropy Roundtable convened an all-day meeting in San Francisco to discuss how charitable foundations could best help solve the growing economic and ecological crisis in America's Pacific Coast fisheries. Roundtable president Adam Meyerson offered four premises underlying the conference in his opening remarks. There are solutions; the search for the solutions involves using the best science; markets and property rights are part of the solution; and philanthropists have a key role to play in finding solutions to this great crisis. Representatives for more than 20 foundations that are concerned about Pacific fisheries issues attended the conference. Presenters included marine biologists, economists and commercial fishers.

Most of the presenters agreed that the chief problem with fisheries is that the current system of regulated open-access encourages overfishing and ecological devastation. University of California economist James Wilens offered his "Parable of the Farm" to illustrate the predicament. His parable invited participants to imagine what farming would be like if it were managed like most fisheries are today.

Parable of the Farm

At the beginning of planting season each year, farmers would gather at the borders of Iowa with their tractors and at a signal rush in to plow and plant as much land as they could before the next farmer beat them to it. Since the farmers could not be sure of getting the same plot the next season they wouldn't take care of the land that they did manage to plow that season. Next year, they would buy bigger faster tractors so that they could reach more land and plow it faster than rival

Potential Benefits of IFQs

- Reduced overcapitalization (too many boats and too much gear) in the fishery (little economic incentive to maintain capacity in a fishery beyond what is needed)

- Greater rewards for efficiency, conservation and stewardship (IFQs provide more economic Incentive to support conservative harvest levels that allow fish populations to grow)

- Reduced bycatch (when IFQs apply to catch and there is adequate monitoring)

- More efficient use of fish products by processors

- When transitioning from a derby fishery, more time to catch fish, resulting in safer working conditions and higher-quality products

- More flexibility to adjust to regulations and other fishing and market conditions

- More economic certainty for fishermen

- Better balance of supply and demand

- Those wanting to leave the fishery would receive some compensation

Pacific Fishery Management Council, "Trawl Rationalization and Individual Fishing Quotas (IFQS)", February 2008.

farmers. Were farming managed this way, the result would be degraded land, excess machinery capacity, the production of low value products, perverse innovation producing bigger, faster tractors, the imposition of more and more detailed regulations and land would have no value. This is exactly what we see in regulated open-access fisheries today. Or as American Enterprise Institute scholar Steven Hayward suggested, "Imagine what the beef industry would look like if it were open access."

Another part of the problem with fisheries is that there is a conflict of visions, according to Washington State University professor of fisheries management Ray Hilborn. On the one hand, fisheries can be valued as marine ecosystems, and on the other, they are seen as resources to generate jobs, food and profit. Hilborn noted that it is impossible to maximize one without harming the other. The problem is how to decide what the proper balance is. Stephen Palumbi, a professor of marine sciences at Stanford University, pointed out that intact marine ecosystems offer other benefits besides harvesting fish. For example, fishing in Monterey, California, yields only $20 million per year, while tourism brings in $2 billion—a lot of that from tourists who come to see marine life. Palumbi argued that establishing marine reserves increases diversity, fishery productivity and tourism.

Participants in the Philanthropy Roundtable conference also heard presentations describing how property rights in fisheries have worked out in a number of areas. Yale University sustainable development economist Robert Repetto described a real life experiment in property rights in the scallop fishery off the Atlantic coast. In the 1980s, Canada adopted essentially a system of tradable quotas in its scallop fishery while the United States maintained a system of top down regulations including ever shorter scallop fishing seasons. Twenty years later the results are stark. The Canadian scallop fishery produces more and bigger scallops and is profitable. On the other hand, Repetto concludes: "If the U.S. scallop fishery were a business, its management would surely be fired, because its revenues could readily be increased by at least 50 percent while its costs were being reduced by an equal percentage. No private sector manager could survive with this degree of inefficiency."

Individual Fishing Quotas

Mercatus Center scholar Maurice McTigue, a former New Zealand cabinet minister, detailed how New Zealand's successful program of individual tradable quotas (ITQs) in its fisheries was established. The result is that fisheries are being sustainably harvested and the export value of their products went up 400 percent. And Mark Lundsten, a former Alaska halibut and sablefish fisher, described how the creation of individual fishing quotas (IFQs) in Alaska transformed those fisheries. In 1994, before (IFQs) the halibut fishing season was a "derby" (called that because it was reminiscent of demolition derbies) lasting 72 hours. After IFQs were assigned, the season lasted 245 days. Fishers did not have to go out in bad weather and consumers got fresh rather than frozen fish. Inevitably establishing property rights in fisheries means that many fishers and boats will have to leave the industry. This fact always generates a lot of initial resistance among fishers.

Representatives from the Bradley Fund for the Environment, the Gordon and Betty Moore Foundation, the Keith Campbell Foundation for the Environment, and the David and Lucille Packard Foundation also briefly described their fisheries programs. Their programs range from encouraging the creation of dedicated access privileges (ITQs are an example) to helping establish territorial use rights in fishing (TURFs) for sea urchin fisheries, and to creating international certification systems for sustainable fisheries such as the Marine Stewardship Council. The foundations also support scientific research on the effects of fishing on marine ecosystems.

Annually, there is $32 billion loss on worldwide fisheries revenues of $100 billion. Clearly the current situation in our fisheries cannot continue. While not a panacea, property rights will be a vital part of the solution to restoring fisheries and marine ecosystems to health.

| *"[Individual Fishing Quotas] have failed to halt overfishing."*

Individual Fishing Quotas Do Not Benefit U.S. Fisheries

Food & Water Watch

Individual Fishing Quotas (IFQs), the permission to catch a percentage of the total allowable catch, have failed to reduce overfishing, argues Food & Water Watch in the following viewpoint. The nation's fisheries are a national resource that should be managed by the federal government for the benefit of the American public, the author maintains. IFQs, however, privatize fishing rights for the benefit of those who own the quotas, Food & Water Watch asserts. When IFQs are taken out of the hands of local communities and consolidated into the hands of big businesses, small coastal communities suffer. Food & Water Watch supports sustainable, local fishing rights.

As you read, consider the following questions:

1. Who really loses as a result of the practice of "gifting" IFQs, in the view of Food & Water Watch?

2. What examples of quota consolidation in IFQ programs does the author provide?

3. What is "price dumping," according to the author?

The Individual Fishing Quota [IFQ] system is a management tool that privatizes and consolidates fishing rights under the guise of reducing overfishing. It has largely failed to address overfishing but has succeeded in consolidating the right to fish. Congress placed a moratorium on the creation of new IFQ programs from 1996–2002 to further assess their implications.

Once the moratorium expired, some of the regional fishery management councils began looking at ways to implement individual fishing quotas in their regions. Problems associated with IFQs remain and cannot be ignored. . . . Congress must acknowledge the inherent public trust, environmental and socioeconomic consequences of IFQ programs.

Issues of Public Trust

When a nation's resource is a public trust, then it is the duty of the federal government to manage that resource for the benefit of the entire public. When a public resource is privatized, the benefits are no longer enjoyed by the public, but rather by those few who now own the resource.

Because the initial quota allocation is awarded to only a handful already participating in the fishery and who have historically caught the most, millions of dollars of a public resource are handed to a lucky few while anyone else who wants to be involved in the fishery has to purchase quota from an initial quota holder.

Although this practice, known as "gifting," is extremely unfair to new fishermen trying to enter the industry or others who never received an initial allocation, the real losers are the public who foot the bill for the continued management of those who have been given the ownership of a public resource.

The National Marine Fisheries Service's requested budget is $727.9 million for 2006, with hundreds of millions of this

"These fish quotas are getting ridiculous."

allocated to programs attempting to ensure the sustainability of fisheries as well as enforcement of current laws and safety at sea. This figure does not include other land and air patrols by the Coast Guard, Bureau of Customs and Border Protection, Civil Air Patrol or state enforcement agencies.

Under this system, it is the taxpayer who pays for the preservation of fisheries. Therefore, if the public pays for the preservation of a public resource, the resource should be just that—public. However, under the system of IFQs, that is not so.

A Property Right

Although IFQs are legally defined as a revocable privilege, they are in actuality treated as a property right. The two basic elements of private property are permanent title and the ability to buy and sell. If quota holders have property rights, they can pursue compensation in court as a "taking" under the Fifth Amendment to the Constitution if any attempt is made to reduce the value of the property.

This has serious ramifications for setting an appropriate total allowable catch [TAC]. The TAC sets a limit on the amount of fish that can be caught within a fishery to ensure overfishing does not decimate fish populations. There is already political pressure to set TACs at levels beyond maximum sustainable yield. If a TAC limit requires a reduction so that a population can rebuild, IFQ holders can respond with legal action. Because these claims could cost the federal government millions of dollars, the government may forgo imposing important conservation measures.

Such a lawsuit was brought in New Zealand, when the government tried to reduce the TAC for the depleting red snapper population. Industry responded with a series of legal actions to prevent the reductions and tried to collect compensation in the case the reductions occur. While the New Zealand Court of Appeals eventually dismissed industry's claims, some U.S. decisions have upheld IFQs as property rights. For example, in both the Johns vs. Johns and the McGee vs. McGee divorce cases in Alaska, both spouses were awarded part of the quota shares in the settlements.

The Socioeconomic Impacts

The quotas are often granted to those with the largest historic catch and then can be resold to the highest bidder—this often means big businesses far from the ocean, far from the fish.

Young fishermen have an even harder time entering the fishery, unless they want to be a sharecropper to big business. All the while, big business has the influence to ensure that privatization and consolidation are legislated at the regional level.

Concentration of market power and the ability to manipulate prices through consolidation of quota has become a significant problem. As quota is increasingly bought up by a small number of companies, more and more small-scale fishermen are left in the cold, leaving coastal communities struggling for survival.

There are countless examples of quota consolidation in IFQ programs. In 2002, the Government Accountability Office [GAO] reported that quota ownership in the surf clam and ocean quahog industry in the Mid-Atlantic was twice as concentrated as the National Marine Fisheries Service data suggested due to different quota holders belonging to a single corporation. The GAO concluded that one entity alone controlled 27 percent of the quota.

In another case, the initial allocation of the halibut-sablefish program, 40 recipients received an average quota of $2.5 million while the lower 4,000 recipients received quota averaging a mere $10,000.

Consolidation of fishing quota comes with negative impacts on small coastal communities. Social costs appear in the form of job losses, reduced incomes, high unemployment rates, rupture of personal relations, loss of professional knowledge and expertise, loss of a traditional culture and a wider gap of income between those who receive the most quota and those who do not.

So, while there are reduced employment opportunities for crew, captains and shore support workers, the windfall profits go to a select few at the initial allocation of the quota, many of who don't even fish, but rather charge others to use the quota.

The Environmental Impacts

First and foremost, Magnuson-Stevens Fishery Conservation and Management Act was intended to "provide for the conservation" of fisheries. Despite this, IFQ programs are often the antithesis of conservation.

To start, such a single species system only values commercially exploited species and does not incorporate broader issues within marine ecosystems. An ecosystem-based approach to fisheries management is the only way to maintain healthy oceans, fish populations and coastal fishing communities.

Proponents of IFQ programs claim that ownership and property rights create an incentive to protect ones' assets, thus to act in the best interest of fish populations and ultimately marine ecosystems. This idea has failed miserably in practice. Once the quota is consolidated into the hands of big business and out of the local communities, the business can then exploit the resource as quickly as possible and then invests the profits where they will grow faster than the depleting fish populations. Once the fish are all gone, the corporation can take its profits and move into a new industry.

Ignoring this issue has led to many environmental problems within fisheries operating under the IFQ system. Because of the very nature of such a system, the incentives to cheat in order to maximize profit off of an existing quota is further decimating marine ecosystems.

One type of cheating is known as "quota busting," which is when fishermen will underreport landings in order to catch more fish than their quota actually allows. This, of course, only further depletes fish populations.

Another practice that is extremely detrimental to the health of fisheries is "high-grading." High-grading refers to the discarding of lower value fish at sea so that they don't count against one's fishing quota. Fish are thrown back into the ocean dead or dying.

"Price dumping" is also a significant problem. This occurs upon reaching shore and discovering that prices are unusually low. Fish are then thrown back into the ocean. This allows quota holders to save their quota for when prices are higher.

All of these methods collectively create a larger problem known as "data fouling," which leads to an underestimation of fishing mortality, making it difficult to accurately set or assess the given TAC.

Considering this, it's of little surprise that IFQs have failed to halt overfishing. Coupled with such dangers as quota busting and high-grading, it is clear that these programs have not achieved conservation goals.

Periodical Bibliography

The following articles have been selected to supplement the diverse views presented in this chapter.

Margaret Bauman "Federal Rule Would Protect Sea Floor Habitat from Bottom Trawling," *Alaska Journal of Commerce*, March 16, 2008.

Hoyt Childers "The 3 Keys to IFQs: Allocation, Allocation, and Allocation," *National Fisherman*, April 2007.

Colin W. Clark "Fisheries Bioeconomics: Why Is It So Widely Misunderstood?" *Population Ecology*, April 2006.

Clive Cookson "Deep-Sea Trawler 'Bandits' Stripping the Oceans, Scientists Warn," *Financial Times*, February 20, 2007.

Economist "The World Needs More Farmed Fish," December 27, 2007.

Rupert Howes "Sustainability Is in Everyone's Interests," Fish Information & Services, People with Opinion, June 15, 2007. www.fis.com/fis/people.

Gary Loverich "Engineer Uses Facts to Bust Bottom-Trawling Myth," *National Fisherman*, January 2007.

Shawn McManus "The Business of IFQs," *National Fisherman*, October 2007.

Gwyn Morgan "Fix the Fishing Industry: Eliminate Subsidies and Stop Destructive Practices," *Globe & Mail* (Toronto), November 26, 2007.

Anna Vinson "Deep Sea Bottom Trawling and the Eastern Tropical Pacific Seascape: A Test Case for Global Action," *Georgetown International Environmental Law Review*, Winter 2006.

Jennifer Weeks "Fish Farming," *CQ Researcher*, July 27, 2007.

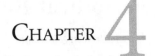

CHAPTER 4

What Impact Do Human Activities Have on Marine Mammals?

Chapter Preface

Oe of several controversies in the debate over the impact of human activities on marine mammals is the threat posed by climate change. Some scientists assert that climate change, induced by human activities such as the use of CO_2-producing fossil fuels, puts Arctic marine mammals in serious danger. The loss of sea ice, for example, creates dramatic shifts in the environment on which these animals depend. According to the editors of *Science Daily*, "Sea ice serves as a platform for resting and reproduction, influences the distribution of food sources, and provides a refuge from predators." Although marine mammals are well adapted to survive the dramatic seasonal changes that the Arctic ecosystem normally undergoes, "the rate and scale of current climate change are expected to distinguish current circumstances from those of the past several millennia. These new conditions present unique challenges to the well-being of Arctic marine mammals," claims marine scientist Sue Moore of the National Oceanic and Atmospheric Administration's Alaska Fisheries Science Center.

In addition to a loss of sea ice, another challenge Arctic marine mammals may face is a significant shift in the availability of prey animals. Polar bears, for example, face a reduction in the quantity of their prey, which will require them to seek alternate food. Unlike other Arctic marine mammal species, such as the beluga whale and bearded seal, which are more opportunistic in their eating habits, polar bears are handicapped by their specific food requirements and hunting techniques, maintains Arctic marine life experts Bodil Bluhm and Rolf Gradinger. As a result, polar bears will experience dramatic changes in their bodies and, in turn, their immune systems. Kathy Burek of Alaska Veterinary Pathology Services adds that climate change may alter the way in which diseases are transmitted across the globe. As a result, Arctic marine mammals will be exposed to new infectious diseases against which they have no defense. These combined impacts due to climate change will put the health of Arctic marine mammals at risk and, worse, threaten their ultimate survival as species.

Other biologists question the link between global warming and species extinction. University of California ecology professor Daniel Botkin challenges the accuracy of predictions that connect climate change to species extinction. He points to what is known as "the Quaternary conundrum." Fossils from the Quaternary period, the last 2.5 million years, fluctuated as glaciers covered the Northern Hemisphere and then retreated. "While current empirical and theoretical ecological forecasts suggest that many species could be at risk from global warming," Botkin explains, "during the recent ice ages few extinctions are documented." North American mammoths, ground sloths, and other large mammals were indeed eliminated during previous rapid climate shifts. However, he claims, human hunters migrating across the Bering Sea land bridge probably played a more significant role in their extinction. "The evidence that global warming will have serious effects on life is thin. Most evidence suggests the contrary," Botkin concludes.

Climate change and its impact on wildlife, including Arctic marine mammals, remains hotly contested. The authors in the following chapter debate the impact of other human activities on marine mammals.

| "Whaling is as indefensible today as it was 60 years ago."

The Commercial Whaling Ban Is Necessary to Protect Endangered Species

Ben Macintyre

Whaling is an indefensible practice, argues Ben Macintyre in the following viewpoint. In fact, he claims, so many people feared whales' extinction that in 1986 the International Whaling Commission banned commercial whaling. Unfortunately, Mcintyre maintains, some nations are hoping to overturn the ban. Claims that killing whales is necessary to study them are absurd, he asserts. Commercial whaling is not an ecologically or economically effective practice, Macintyre concludes. Macintyre, a regular columnist for The Times *of London, is a historical novelist.*

As you read, consider the following questions:

1. According to Macintyre, what other environmental debate does the whaling debate mirror?

Ben Macintyre, "Whale Hunting: A Saga of Cheating, Bribery, and Greed," *The Times* (London), May 10, 2007. Copyright © 2007 Times Newspapers Limited. Reproduced by permission.

2. To what does the author compare the killing of a whale for research?

3. In Macintyre's opinion, from what unnatural causes are whales still dying?

As a child, I sat on a whale every day. Many years before I was born a 50-ton sperm whale had washed up on the Scottish coast near to where I grew up, and one of my relatives had cleverly fashioned a stool out of one of its enormous vertebrae. To a child, that bone-stool was a thing of wonder: a fraction of a creature of impossible vastness. I would scan the sea, imagining the great beast from which my seat had come, dreaming that another whale might one day burst the surface. It never did.

Securing the Whale's Future

My whale (as I considered it) had been found on the beach in 1946. By coincidence, that was also the year 15 whaling countries signed up to a convention "recognising the interests of the nations of the world in safeguarding for future generations the great natural resources represented by the whale stocks". Quite how far those stocks had been depleted was a matter of guesswork, but an estimated two million whales were killed in the 20th century alone. Right-thinking people agreed: continuing to destroy these beautiful, intelligent, ecologically important and seriously endangered mammals was not clever. The International Whaling Commission (IWC) banned commercial whaling in 1986.

The future of the whale should have been secure, yet today the whaling ban is closer to being overturned than at any time in the past 20 years, consensus on whaling is more distant than ever and many whale species remain on the brink of extinction. [In May 2007] the IWC [met] in Alaska with pro-whaling nations, led by Japan, determined to resume the hunt on a commercial scale.

The Whaling Debate

The whaling debate was stranded and picked clean long ago. It is a rotten thing, riddled with bad science, exploited loopholes, petty politicking, bribery, blind nationalism and human greed, both gastronomic and economic. But perhaps more alarming still, the whaling debate bears disturbing parallels with the looming battle over climate change, another issue on which the clarity of science is being hopelessly clouded by politics and narrow self-interest. The world has had 60 years to protect the whale for all time; there is nowhere near that long to find a way to rebalance a warming world.

Japanese tactics in the whaling struggle have been ruthlessly cynical. [In 2006] Japanese whalers killed 853 minke whales and 10 fin whales, and they [started] hunting humpback whales [in 2007]. All were eaten, in the name of "scientific research" that most reputable biologists dismiss as a sham.

Killing a whale for research is like building a coal-fired power station to examine greenhouse gases.

The claim that whales eat lots of fish and thus threaten stocks needed for human consumption has been comprehensively rubbished by scientists: whales and human tend to prey on different fish.

The Japanese campaign to resume whaling is more a matter of national pride than culinary taste. Indeed, whale meat is principally eaten by the older generation in Japan, who turned to it as a foodstuff during postwar shortages. Japan insists that whale meat is a national delicacy; in truth, its relationship to the Japanese palate is closer to our own lingering fondness for Spam [a common staple during WWII]; inexplicable to anyone under the age of 60.

[In 2006] Japan gained a majority on the IWC by recruiting countries to the whaling cause in return for fisheries grants worth millions of dollars. Mongolia, for example, has proved a keen supporter of whaling, despite not having a coastline: Gobi Dick, sadly, has yet to be discovered.

The whalers would need a 75 per cent majority to overturn the ban, but with a single-vote advantage [in 2006] they managed to push through a resolution declaring that the moratorium on whale hunting was no longer necessary. In response, a British diplomatic campaign has rounded up six new member nations to vote against Japan and its allies. What once seemed a moral imperative has become a grubby game of vote-bargaining, which defenders of the whale must play.

Japan insists that whale populations have grown sufficiently to permit a resumption of hunting, but most marine ecologists disagree, pointing out that while some species may be slowly recovering, others are still perilously close to extinction. Whales are still dying from unnatural causes: errant fishing nets, human noise, pollution and continued hunting. No one knows quite how many are left. That is surely the best reason for not killing any more.

The pro-whaling lobby points out that Britain and the US played a big role in the slaughter, while opponents of whaling stand accused of "imperialism" for "imposing moral and ethical judgments that affect our rights to use resources". The argument echoes that of the polluters in China and India, who insist that since the West caused the environmental damage that has led to global warming, we are in no position to lecture others.

An Indefensible Practice

No amount of dodgy science and diplomatic manoeuvring should disguise that whaling is as indefensible today as it was 60 years ago: the unspeakable in pursuit of what is, to most of the world's population, uneatable. Whale-hunting is moribund, inhumane and uneconomic; whale-watching, on the other hand, is profitable, harmless and rapidly expanding.

Today the argument for tackling climate change may seem equally stark, but that too is being swamped by the accusations of nationalism, imperialism and influence-peddling. If we could not combine to defend this single symbolic organism during the past 60 years, what hope is there of finding a working consensus on global warming before it is too late?

Whale oil represented a huge global market in the 19th century, because it burned brightly, was relatively easy to harvest, cheap to process and supplied by nature in apparently endless quantities. The same was once said of oil.

| "Whaling, handled right and in moderation, can be sustainable."

Whaling Can Be Sustainable When Properly Managed

Philip Armour

If conducted in moderation, whaling can be sustainable, claims Philip Armour in the following viewpoint. For example, he asserts, Norwegians sustainably hunt minke whales every summer. Moreover, Armour argues, many whale species are not endangered. If well managed, he maintains, whaling would not deplete whale populations. Indeed, Armour reasons, whales would be better protected by efforts to save the ocean habitat and the ocean life that feeds them. Armour, who writes for Outside *magazine, was once the editor of the magazine's Swedish edition.*

As you read, consider the following questions:

1. What are some of the nations that Armour claims have slipped through loopholes in the whaling ban?
2. In the author's view, for what was the International Whaling Commission founded?
3. In Armour's opinion, how many of the thirty-seven whale species are endangered?

When the International Whaling Commission convenes [in May 2006], its worldwide moratorium on commercial whaling will be under attack. It should be. The time has come for regulations that recognize that whaling, handled right and in moderation, can be sustainable.

The moratorium, in place since 1985, has accomplished a great deal. Most countries, including the United States, have given up whaling, and as a result, many species that were dwindling are now on the rebound.

Slipping Through Loopholes

But there are also loopholes that a handful of persistent whaling nations have managed to slip through. Norway has never recognized the moratorium; Japan and Iceland claim that they kill whales for research, though they sell surplus meat for food. Now these countries are clamoring to hunt larger species and to do so in international waters.

In April 2004, I spent two weeks on the 53-foot Norwegian whaling ship *Sofie*, living with its five-man crew. I saw the Norwegians shoot six minke whales with grenade-tipped harpoons, drag them to the boat and kill them with blasts to the skull from a .458-caliber rifle. Once onboard, the whales dwarfed us all. But at an average of 25 feet and seven tons, the minke is small—for a whale.

There are 120,000 to 182,000 minkes in the North Atlantic. Norwegian whalers hunt them every spring and summer along the fjord-carved coast of Arctic Norway, shooting 639 in 2005 and selling their red, beef-like meat for about $10 a pound. Given the animal's healthy numbers, killing and eating limited numbers of minke whales is sustainable, despite the Norwegian quota increase to 1,052 whales for 2006.

Whalers cite success with the minke programs to make their case for going after larger, more profitable species. But minkes have never been heavily hunted; as a result, their num-

A Different View of Whales

Not everyone romanticizes about the ocean-going behemoths. From Japan to Scandinavia and even among Alaska's Native Americans, whales are often seen merely as giant meat and oil factories, triggering a furious intercultural debate over commercial whaling. . . .

Japan and Norway contend that whale populations have grown to the point that some species are no longer at risk of extinction and should be open to hunting.

Mary H. Cooper, CQ Researcher, *August 2, 2002.*

bers far exceed those of larger whales like humpback or fin, two species Japan plans to hunt in 2006.

Whaling Commission's Purpose

For its part, the International Whaling Commission, which is essentially a trade organization founded to preserve whale numbers for future hunting—not for conservation—is predisposed to serve whalers, not the public good. That's why it has failed to come up with a nuanced framework that can accommodate both environmental and economic needs.

The commission focuses on specific whale numbers rather than on general ocean health. But the old saw that all whales are in danger of extinction simply isn't true. Seven of the mammal's 37 species are still endangered, but only two are in serious trouble. Environmentalists need not bother with saving every whale. They'd be better off coming up with a plan to save the oceans.

Whales can become endangered by the loss of other ocean life that sustains them; and when whales are hunted, rather than allowed to die from natural causes and feed back into the ecosystem, that endangers the habitat, which in turn endangers whales. The debate over how to save the whales, therefore, needs to focus on both whaling and ocean health.

With proper management, whaling need not cause extinctions or deplete ecosystems, but as it stands, the fox is guarding the chicken coop. Whales need at least 50 more years to repopulate before hunting of larger species should resume. The commission, however, has proven incapable of allowing stocks to replenish fully, as we've seen with the moratorium's sloppy loopholes. Moreover, whaling nations have allegedly influenced the votes of commission members in exchange for development aid.

A more disinterested body needs to govern whale hunting, and I suggest the United Nations. Fifty years would give the United Nations time to configure a global fishing commission—and the International Whaling Commission time to dismantle. Limited whaling of certain species would continue, while the others would be given a rest. Conservation is the best option not just for the environment, but for the fishing industry as well. Whaling, however distasteful, needs to be reinvented with global resources—not just whales—in mind.

"Sonar [is] harming the ability of 71 types of whales, dolphins, and porpoises to communicate, navigate, and hunt."

Antisubmarine Sonar Harms Marine Mammals

Dick Russell

Antisubmarine sonar hinders the ability of marine mammals to communicate, navigate, and hunt, maintains Dick Russell in the following viewpoint. Scientists originally thought sonar simply misdirected marine mammals, leading them to beach, he claims. Modern studies have found, however, that sonar damages the organs and tissue of marine mammals, Russell asserts. Nevertheless, he argues, the military remains exempt from provisions of the Marine Mammal Protection Act that would prevent the threat sonar poses to these sensitive marine mammals. Russell is a longtime sport fisherman, environmental journalist, and author of Striper Wars: An American Fish Story.

As you read, consider the following questions:

1. According to Russell, why has the navy been forced to acknowledge the connection between sonar and whale strandings?

2. What are the limitations of the navy pledge to reduce sonar power when marine mammals are spotted, in the author's view?

3. What has the Natural Resources Defense Council demanded that the navy understand, according to Russell?

The pilot whales began coming ashore [in January 2006], on North Carolina's Cape Hatteras National Seashore, not far from Whalebone Junction, where fishermen make the turn toward the marina at Oregon Inlet. Short-finned with distinctly rounded heads and long, stocky dark bodies, some were almost 20 feet long, weighing up to three tons. By the time they were discovered in the surf near a lonely five-mile stretch of beach, 15 pilot whales—6 of them pregnant—were dead. Seven more had to be euthanized by veterinarians. During the next two days, a newborn minke whale and two dwarf sperm whales also died in one of the largest beaching events ever documented along this coastline.

Examining Possible Causes

Scientists arrived to gather tissue; after the necropsies, the whales were buried on the beach. "It's curious to have three different kinds of whales strand, and a number of possible causes are being examined. Sonar is certainly one of them," said Connie Barclay, spokeswoman for the National Oceanic and Atmospheric Administration [NOAA].

On the day the strandings began, several Navy ships conducted submarine-hunting exercises off North Carolina's Outer Banks, using loudspeakers to send mid-frequency sonar sound waves across ten or even a hundred miles of ocean. Sonar devices can locate an enemy's sophisticated, almost-silent diesel submarines by, ironically, making a deafening noise—sometimes above 230 decibels, as loud as a Saturn V rocket blasting off. (Underwater noise of only 120 decibels—a level billions of times less intense—has been known to disrupt whale behavior.)

Whales Under Assault

Despite the end of the era of mass whale slaughter, the general degradation of the oceans has left whales under assault as never before. At a moment when scientists are, for the first time, becoming aware of the complexities of whale societies, those societies are being threatened by a growth of ocean noise that could prevent whales from locating one another and finding food. The point is that very little is known about the broader effects of sound on whales, and even as large amounts of research money are going toward fine-tuning the effects of sonar or, increasingly, conducting oil and gas seismic surveys, far too little is devoted to . . . basic science.

Peter Canby, OnEarth, *Spring 2007.*

The Navy maintains that the sonar training had nothing to do with the whale strandings, but it has been forced to acknowledge such problems in the past. In 2000, 16 whales, of three species, beached themselves along a 150-mile stretch of the Bahamas; whales and porpoises have also come ashore and died on five different occasions on the Canary Islands, as well as along the coasts of Greece, Spain, and Alaska. Each time, sonar exercises were being conducted by the U.S. Navy or NATO [North Atlantic Treaty Organization] forces nearby. In a 2004 report, the Scientific Committee of the International Whaling Commission found that the evidence linking Navy sonar and whale strandings "appears overwhelming." In November [2005], a U.N. report concurred that increased naval military maneuvers and sonar are harming the ability of 71 types of whales, dolphins, and porpoises to communicate, navigate, and hunt.

Nor, as once thought, does the sonar simply misdirect the animals to beach by interfering with their echolocation. Scientists have detected severe lesions in organ tissue, bleeding in the brain and from the ears, and indications that the whales have been literally shaken apart by the intense sound. The journal *Nature* has reported that the victims of one mass stranding exhibited strange gas bubbles in certain organs. This has led researchers to conclude that the whales may have suffered a kind of decompression sickness similar to "the bends," known to kill human divers who surface too quickly. Pilot whales and dwarf sperm whales dive more than 1,000 feet deep to feed off the slopes of the continental shelf such as those off of North Carolina. The whales at Cape Hatteras may have panicked and come up too fast.

Reducing Sonar's Impact

Yet now, roughly 60 miles farther down the Carolina coast, the Navy plans more than 160 sonar exercises annually across a 500-square-mile area at a new Undersea Warfare Training Range. The Navy has pledged to reduce sonar power should any marine mammals be spotted within 350 yards of its ships or 200 yards of helicopters towing sonar arrays—but that accounts only for animals on the surface, and some whales that died in the Bahamas are thought to have been tens of miles away from the sonar source.

In 2003, the Natural Resources Defense Council (NRDC) got the courts to severely restrict the Navy's plan to deploy a new low-frequency active (LFA) sonar system around the globe. The intensity level of LFA is basically the same as mid-frequency sonar, but because it operates in a lower frequency, it covers a lot more ocean. The [George W.] Bush administration responded by pushing legislation through Congress that exempts the military from key provisions of the Marine Mammal Protection Act. In essence, the Navy can now choose whether or not to abide by the act. In October [2005], the

NRDC and several other conservation groups sued the Navy over mid-range frequency sonar, demanding that it "understand the environmental impacts of its actions, and to mitigate those impacts, before flooding vast areas of marine habitat with intense, harmful noise."

Whales' ability to withstand this new variety of human onslaught remains very much an open question. Meanwhile, Japan, Norway, and Iceland continue to flout a 1986 international moratorium on commercial whaling. In early November [2005], a Japanese fleet left for Antarctica with plans to kill more than 900 minke whales and 10 endangered fin whales. [In 2006], Japan plans to kill 50 humpback whales. Whales are taken under the guise of "scientific research," but the meat quickly reaches Japanese supermarkets and restaurants.

And so, nearly 30 years after sending its little Zodiacs to confront Soviet whaling ships and sparking the environmental movement, Greenpeace is going back at it too, with plans to disrupt the Japanese whale hunt in the Southern Ocean.

> "The Navy implements twenty-nine pro-
> tective measures . . . [that] afford sig-
> nificant protection to marine mammals
> while maintaining [sonar] training fi-
> delity."

Antisubmarine Sonar Has Adequate Safeguards to Protect Marine Mammals

Donald C. Winter

The navy is a good environmental steward, claims Secretary of the Navy Donald C. Winter in the following viewpoint. In fact, he asserts, the navy has implemented numerous protective measures to protect marine mammals during sonar training exercises. Sonar detects hostile submarines that are equipped with modern silencing technologies so that they would otherwise go undetected and put American lives at risk, Winter argues. To protect national security, he maintains, the navy must train personnel in the use of navy sonar before they are deployed to detect and combat hostile submarines.

Donald C. Winter, "Testimony before the Senate Armed Services Committee in The Secretary of the Navy's FY 2009 Posture Statement," February 28, 2008.

As you read, consider the following questions:

1. In Winter's opinion, what is necessary if the navy is to respond swiftly and decisively anywhere in the world?

2. What facts support the author's claim that the dimension of international commerce is ever increasing?

3. In Winter's view, why was the navy offered alternative arrangements for compliance with the National Environmental Policy Act?

Today our Nation is faced with a myriad of challenges and uncertainties across the globe. There have been several unexpected, and sometimes sudden, changes in the security environment over the past few years. Yet many of the strategic imperatives of the United States—particularly with respect to the maritime environment—remain unchanged. It is clear the United States must have the capacity to act in such a fluid and unpredictable environment, and that Naval forces offer unique flexibility to respond swiftly and decisively anywhere in the world. Providing this flexibility requires that the Department of the Navy invest wisely across a wide range of capabilities, and that we take care to deliver a balanced portfolio of capabilities to the Joint force. Worldwide presence, credible deterrence and dissuasion, projection of power from naval platforms anywhere on the globe, and the ability to prevail at sea are the critical, most fundamental elements of the Navy and Marine Corps strategic posture; these are our indispensable contributions to the joint warfighting capability of the Nation.

The United States is a maritime power, bounded by sea to the east and west. The health of our national economy depends on assuring safe transit through the seas—and the maritime dimension of international commerce is ever increasing. Consider that 70 percent of the earth is covered by water, 80 percent of the world's population lives in close proximity to the coast, and 90 percent of the world's international commerce is transported via the sea. Given our national interests,

Monitoring Marine Life

[The U.S. Navy's surveillance system known as SURTASS LFA uses] three monitoring techniques:

- Visual monitoring for marine mammals and sea turtles from the SURTASS LFA sonar vessel during daylight hours;

- Passive (low frequency) SURTASS array to listen for sounds generated by marine mammals as an indicator of their presence; and

- High frequency (HF) active sonar to detect/locate/track potentially affected marine mammals (and possibly sea turtles) near the SURTASS LFA sonar vessel and the sound field produced by the SURTASS LFA sonar source array.

Department of the U.S. Navy, 2007.

and the role we play in the world, it is unsurprising that our Sailors and Marines are constantly called upon to react to a wide range of challenges. I suggest that the strength of a nation's naval force remains an essential measure of that nation's status and role in the world. I also submit that maritime dominance by the United States remains vital to our national security, to our position in the world, and to our ability to defend and promote our interests. . . .

Marine Mammals and Active Sonar

The most critical readiness issue relates to the Navy's ability to train using active sonar while minimizing the effect on marine mammals. One of the most challenging threats that our Naval forces face is modern, quiet diesel-electric submarines. These submarines employ state-of-the-art silencing technologies and other advances, such as special hull treatments, that make them almost undetectable with passive sonar and also reduce their vulnerability to detection with active sonar. A diesel-electric submarine so equipped can covertly operate in coastal and open ocean areas, blocking Navy access to combat zones and increasing United States vessels' vulnerability to torpedo and anti-ship missile attacks. Currently, over 40 countries operate more than 300 diesel-electric submarines worldwide, including potential adversaries in the Asia-Pacific and Middle East areas. Naval strike groups are continuously deployed to these high-threat areas. Training with the use of mid-frequency active (MFA) sonar is a vital component of pre-deployment training. The tactical use of MFA sonar is the best means of detecting potentially hostile, quiet, diesel-electric submarines. The inability to train effectively with active sonar literally puts the lives of thousands of Americans at risk.

In January 2008, a federal district court issued an injunction precluding the Navy's ability to train effectively with MFA in critical exercises scheduled to occur in the Southern California Operating Area through January 2009, creating an unacceptable risk that strike groups may not be certified for deployment in support of world-wide operational and combat activities. Because the Composite Unit Training Exercises and the Joint Task Force Exercises off Southern California are critical to the ability to deploy strike groups ready for combat, the President concluded that continuing to train with MFA in these exercises is in the paramount interest of the United States and granted a temporary exemption from the requirements of the Coastal Zone Management Act for use of MFA sonar in these exercises through January 2009. Additionally, due to the emergency circumstances created by an injunction that would prevent the Navy from reliably training and certifying strike groups ready for deployment, the Council on Environmental Quality (CEQ) authorized, and the Navy accepted, alternative arrangements for compliance with the National Environmental Policy Act. Despite these developments, the trial court refused to set aside the injunction. As a result the Navy has appealed the court's refusal to give effect to the President's and CEQ's actions by dissolving the injunction and the court's failure to properly tailor the injunction in the first place to allow the Navy to train effectively. . . .

A Good Steward

The Department continues to be a good steward of the environment, while providing the necessary training that is essential to national security and ensures the safety of our people. The Department is engaged in a comprehensive effort to ensure compliance with the National Environmental Policy Act, Marine Mammal Protection Act, Endangered Species Act, Coastal Zone Management Act, National Marine Sanctuaries Act, and Executive Order 12114. Twelve EISs [environmental impact statements] are in development with associated Records of Decision (ROD) scheduled for issuance by the end of calendar year 2009. The Navy implements twenty-nine protective measures developed in conjunction with the National Marine Fisheries Service, the Federal regulator responsible for oversight and implementation of the Marine Mammal Protection Act. These measures afford significant protection to marine mammals while maintaining training fidelity. The Navy has steadily increased funding for marine mammal research from $12 million in 2006 to $18 million in 2008 and 2009. The Navy's financial commitment constitutes more than half of the world-wide funding for research on the effects of anthropogenic sound on marine mammals. Over the past several years, tremendous progress has been made in expanding the scientific base of knowledge, especially concerning the species identified as the most sensitive to mid-frequency active sonar, deep diving beaked whales. The Navy, working with the National Marine Fisheries Service, is engaged in a three-year controlled exposure study of sound on whales at the Navy's Atlantic Undersea Test and Evaluation Center in the Bahamas. This study, along with other research, development, test and evaluation efforts, will provide further information needed to understand and effectively mitigate the effects of active sonar on marine mammals.

"We should ... recognize that teaching whales and dolphins to perform tricks does not showcase their abilities—it exploits them."

Keeping Marine Mammals in Captivity Is Cruel Exploitation

Humane Society of the United States

Keeping marine mammals in captivity to perform tricks is entertainment, not education, argues the Humane Society of the United States (HSUS) in the following viewpoint. The process of capturing marine mammals for these modern sideshows is brutal, HSUS claims. For example, animals are driven into shallow water, and frantic mothers are separated from their young, HSUS maintains. Moreover, the claim that in a degrading environment marine mammals are safer in captivity discourages efforts to protect them and their habitat, the author asserts. HSUS is an organization dedicated to the protection and care of animals.

As you read, consider the following questions:

1. According to HSUS, what did people learn about whales and dolphins in the 1960s?

2. What evidence does the author provide that the trauma of capturing marine mammals is real?

3. To what animal does the dolphinaria industry frequently compare dolphins, in the opinion of HSUS?

At the turn of the last century, showmen like P.T. Barnum exhibited exotic and "freakish" animals for the amusement and amazement of their customers. Barnum displayed the first captive whale, in fact—a beluga whale from the Arctic. The animal, held in a small box filled with water as a sideshow at Barnum's circus, lived only a few months. But the idea caught on, and by the end of the century, trained whales and dolphins, leaping and spinning to entertain wide-eyed spectators, were on display in dolphinaria from Belgium to South Africa and from the United States to Japan.

Justifying Exploitation

In the last 100 years, the global community has made significant progress on the issue of animal cruelty. There are anticruelty and humane slaughter laws in many countries now. Yet the practice of keeping whales and dolphins in water-filled boxes, started by a huckster who callously exploited animals for profit, persists. The boxes are bigger. The water is cleaner. The food is better. The training methods are kinder. But the concept—capturing intelligent, socially complex, wide-ranging animals from the wild and confining them for the public's amusement and amazement—is basically the same.

In Barnum's day, profit alone justified the capture and confinement of whales and dolphins. In the 1960s, with the popularity of the television program *Flipper* and the rise of the environmental movement, the public learned that whales and dolphins were intelligent and social creatures. People became uncomfortable with dolphinaria whose sole motive was entertainment and profit. The dolphinarium industry had to come up with a better raison d'être. The themes of education and conservation had great potential to justify the continuation of what was, in essence, an archaic and exploitative practice. Unfortunately, the public's love affair with these graceful and intriguing ocean mammals is so intense that people seem reluctant to look beyond the glossy surface of the new philosophy to the unchanged reality beneath.

Most captive whales and dolphins have been captured from the wild. Breeding these species in captivity has been largely a hit-and-miss affair. Only the orca and the bottlenose dolphin have been bred with any significant success. Some species have had only a few successful births, while others are no longer held in captivity because they simply did not survive when confined. However, despite their relative breeding success, orcas and bottlenose dolphins do not have self-sustaining captive populations. Both species are still captured from the wild, especially when dolphinaria in the developing world need to increase their "collections."

A Violent Affair

Capture is a violent affair. Animals are herded toward shore into shallow water, or chased by catcher boats. When driving the animals to shore, capture operators ruthlessly separate juveniles (those still swimming with their mothers but no longer dependent on milk) from frantic females, truss them in a sling, and carry them from the water to a transport vehicle. When chasing animals, capture operators either encircle them with nets or use specially designed lassoes on bow-riding individuals, before dragging them on board. In Canada, men actually jump on the backs of belugas in shallow water and "ride" them to exhaustion in a traumatic "rodeo." The trauma is real; in an analysis of a U.S. government-maintained database, researchers found that mortality rates for bottlenose dolphins shoot up six-fold immediately after a capture. The rate only drops back down after about 35 to 45 days.

Sending the Wrong Message

Visitors to marine amusement parks are fascinated by the intelligence, sensitivity and grace of dolphins and whales. Yet many people don't realize the degree of suffering and injustice involved in taking these animals from their families and native habitats, holding them captive in highly artificial and unnatural environments.

Marine parks and aquariums claim to educate, but in reality they teach people that the capture and exploitation of these intelligent and complex creatures is acceptable. They send a message that the whole of nature is ours to exploit, for a reason as frivolous as sheer entertainment. That's why many scientists and experts . . . , oppose all captivity of marine mammals.

In Defense of Animals, USA, "The Case Against Captivity."

Most disturbingly, this spike in mortality occurs every time dolphins are transported. Each time they are confined and shipped from one place to another, it is as traumatic as if they were being newly captured from the wild. The experience of being removed from water and restrained is apparently so stressful to dolphins that they never find it routine. This is in marked contrast to other wild mammals (including other marine mammals such as sea lions), who eventually acclimate to the transport process.

Captive dolphin husbandry has apparently improved over the years, again based on analyses of this U.S. database. As noted above, bigger tanks, better water quality, and healthier food, as well as some progress in veterinary medicine, have allowed captive dolphins to live longer in captivity. In "the old days," captive dolphins rarely lived more than a few years. The dolphinaria industry calls this improvement a "learning curve," a phrase that obscures the fact that animals died prematurely for decades while people figured out how to care for them.

In the last dozen years or so, captive dolphins began living about as long as their wild counterparts. Given that dolphinaria emphasize that their captives are safe from predators and pollution, receive regular veterinary care, and do not suffer from food shortages, the failure of captive dolphins to routinely live longer than wild dolphins is significant. Many wildlife species live longer in zoos—they have greater quantity of life, regardless of quality of life. This is especially true of prey species who, despite their confinement in cages or pens, at least are spared from becoming a predator's lunch. However, captive bottlenose dolphins live as long as their wild cousins, but not longer. Orcas live significantly shorter lives in captivity. If sharks, habitat degradation, and starvation do not kill captive dolphins, what does?

Captivity Is Not Safer

Dolphinaria cannot have it both ways—either captivity is safer than the wild (therefore captive dolphins should routinely live longer than wild dolphins) or there are factors acting on captive dolphins that simply replace causes of mortality found in the natural environment. One possible factor is stress, suggested by the number of captive dolphins who die of infections (stress is known to lower immune response in many mammals, including humans). Dolphin medicine is still relatively primitive; dolphins, with their perpetual smiles, often do not exhibit recognizable symptoms of illness, such as lost appetite, until they are near death. Veterinary care may thus be a poor exchange for natural habitat when it comes to maintaining dolphin health.

There is a movement in the animal-protection community urging dolphinaria to return captive whales and dolphins to the wild. Some individuals are not good candidates for release—they are injured, chronically ill, very old, or simply too timid in personality. But others could probably survive, and survive well, if allowed to once again become self-sufficient. The dolphinaria industry strongly opposes this movement. Since several species of endangered wildlife have been successfully reintroduced to the wild, this opposition seems to arise more from economic than conservation concerns. In voicing their opposition, dolphinaria frequently claim that captive dolphins are like domesticated dogs (implying that "abandoning" them would be cruel) and that natural habitats are so degraded that dolphins are better off in human care.

Whales and dolphins are not domesticated. They are naturally benign toward people, a characteristic ruthlessly exploited by P.T. Barnum's entrepreneurial descendants. But they have not been selectively bred for generations to become dependent on humans. With proper and careful rehabilitation, many wild-caught captive whales and dolphins could undoubtedly relearn the survival skills they were taught as calves, no matter how long they have been held in captivity. Captivity dulls their independence but does not necessarily destroy it.

As for claiming that releasing wildlife into degraded habitat is cruel, this is hardly a good conservation message. Many people might feel that saving the natural environment is hopeless or beside the point after hearing such a message. They might think that the only safe place for dolphins (or any other wildlife) is in captivity. With such an attitude, habitat degradation will merely continue, with more populations of whales and dolphins put at risk of extinction. The solution to habitat degradation is to clean up the habitat, not remove wildlife from it. Zoos and aquaria are not Noah's Ark—such a concept is unrealistic and dangerously counterproductive to effective conservation.

The world should not enter the 21st century clinging to archaic 20th century practices. We should shed the mantle of the exploitative and greedy sideshow barker and recognize that teaching whales and dolphins to perform tricks does not showcase their abilities—it exploits them. These circus acts are not educational—they are entertainment. And out-dated entertainment at that. Dolphins do not belong in captivity in the new century. They belong where they have lived for millennia, in the ocean, where their continued presence will motivate us to protect them.

"Knowledge acquired through research using husbandry data from animals in public display facilities . . . is essential to marine mammal conservation."

Keeping Marine Mammals in Captivity Promotes Conservation

Alliance of Marine Mammal Parks and Aquariums

Marine mammal parks and aquariums help educate people about the importance of marine mammal conservation, asserts the Alliance of Marine Mammal Parks and Aquariums (AMMPA) in the following viewpoint. AMMPA members have improved the success of marine mammal reproduction and promote research that benefits the health and welfare of marine mammals, AMMPA maintains. Moreover, marine parks and aquariums provide a place where once-stranded animals can be rehabilitated and eventually released. AMMPA is committed to high standards of care for marine mammals and promotes their conservation.

As you read, consider the following questions:

1. What does the collective membership of AMMPA represent, according to the author?
2. What are the most common species exhibited by AMMPA members?
3. In the opinion of AMMPA, what is one of the most effective ways of ensuring the health of wild marine mammal populations in the twenty-first century?

The Alliance of Marine Mammal Parks and Aquariums is an international association representing marine life parks, aquariums, zoos, research facilities, and professional organizations dedicated to the highest standards of care for marine mammals and to their conservation in the wild through public education, scientific study, and wildlife presentations. It was founded in 1987 and established offices near Washington, DC, in 1992, when it was formally incorporated. Collectively, the Alliance membership represents the greatest body of experience and knowledge about marine mammal care and husbandry.

The Alliance is the first and largest organization in the U.S. or abroad dedicated to the concerns and issues that affect the public display of marine mammals. The most commonly exhibited species in Alliance member facilities are dolphins, beluga and killer whales, sea lions and seals.

The Alliance administers a stringent accreditation process for its members. Accredited members must uphold Alliance Standards and Guidelines to optimize the psychological and physical health of, and environmental conditions for, individual marine mammals under their care, and to maximize the educational and scientific value of their collections as a whole.

A Top Priority

Education is a top priority of Alliance members, who are committed to programming aimed at teachers, children, and

Attitudes Toward Marine Life Parks

- 97 percent of respondents agree that marine life parks, aquariums and zoos play an important role in educating the public about marine mammals they might not otherwise have the chance to see.

- 96 percent agree that marine life parks, aquariums and zoos provide people with valuable information about the importance of oceans, waters and the animals that live there.

- 93 percent agree that visiting a marine life park, aquarium or zoo can inspire conservation action that can help marine mammals and their natural environment.

- 93 percent agree that people are more likely to be concerned about animals if they learn about them at marine life parks, aquariums and zoos.

- If looking for educational information about marine mammals, 75 percent would either visit a marine life park, aquarium or zoo or go to their Web sites.

Harris Interactive, on behalf of AMMPA,
September 16–21, 2004.

adults. These programs enhance the experience of seeing living animals with exhibits, displays, programs, publications, and other learning tools. Education programs provide opportunities for visitors to learn about marine mammal biology and natural history and become more aware of, and sensitive toward, the marine environment. They also address important marine conservation issues and engender a strong, active commitment to marine mammal conservation for which the public must ultimately shoulder the responsibility.

Alliance member collaborations have continually enhanced the success of dolphin and whale reproduction as members share information and provide technical assistance important to reproduction management. The Alliance also, when requested, facilitates partnering agreements between individual members to enhance breeding and genetic diversity.

The Alliance emphasizes and promotes research that benefits the health and well-being of both the marine mammals living in public display facilities and those in the wild. Knowledge acquired through research using husbandry data from animals in public display facilities, in tandem with field research, is essential to marine mammal conservation and one of the most effective ways of ensuring the health of wild marine mammal populations in the 21st century.

The Alliance supports the voluntary participation of its members in activities aimed at:

- rescuing, rehabilitating, and releasing stranded marine mammals

- providing homes to animals that are deemed non-releasable, and

- collecting stranded animal data, which is a significant source of information on the natural history, health, and status of wild populations.

Caring for stranded marine mammals is a critical commitment and the accumulated knowledge, collective experience, and resources of Alliance facilities are the primary factors in the many successful rehabilitation efforts each year.

Periodical Bibliography

The following articles have been selected to supplement the diverse views presented in this chapter.

Tom Arrandale — "Disappearing Species," *CQ Researcher*, November 30, 2007.

Peter Canby — "Deadly Sonar: The U.S. Navy Bears Down on Whales—and the Scientists Who Study Them," *OnEarth*, Spring 2007.

Elizabeth Chang — "Should You Swim with This Dolphin?" *Washington Post*, January 1, 2006.

Earth Island Journal — "Watershed for Whales," Autumn 2007.

Geoff Fein — "At-Sea Sonar Training Vital for Maintaining Sub-Hunting Skills," *Defense Daily*, February 25, 2008.

David Helvarg — "A Dolphin Disses War," *AlterNet*, April 11, 2003. www.alternet.org.

Monica Medina — "Japan Should Stop the Charade of Killing Whales for 'Science,'" *Seattle Times*, January 16, 2008.

Kristen Noel — "Navy Invests in Protecting Marine Mammals," *All Hands*, February 2008.

David Perlman — "Big Drop in Gray Whale Population Suggests Ocean Is in Trouble," *San Francisco Chronicle*, September 11, 2007.

Brenda Peterson — "Ludicrous Dolphin Plan Shows We Are Scared Silly," *Seattle Post-Intelligencer*, February 18, 2007.

Joshua Reichert — "We Need to Save the Whales—Again," *Baltimore Sun*, May 31, 2006.

For Further Discussion

Chapter 1

1. The Bahá'í International Community claims that although humanity depends on ocean health, human activities have put the oceans' health at risk. Jack Sterne and David Wilmot agree that the world's oceans are threatened but argue that those who use the oceans can inspire policies that will improve ocean health. Do you think Sterne and Wilmot's strategies are sufficient to bring about the shared responsibility that the Bahá'í International Community believes is necessary to restore the health of the world's oceans? Why or why not?

2. Peter N. Spotts maintains that carbon-dioxide emissions, overfishing, global warming, and toxic runoff seriously threaten the world's coral reefs. Timothy R.E. Keeney contends that organizations such as the National Oceanic and Atmospheric Administration have taken significant steps to reduce these impacts and protect coral reefs. What evidence does each author provide to support his claim. Which evidence do you find more persuasive? Explain, citing from the viewpoints.

3. According to Ben Carmichael, current fishing practices will soon lead to the collapse of many commercial fisheries. Jim Hutchinson Jr. disputes this claim, arguing that the interpretation of the statistics cited by those who predict the collapse is inaccurate. If Hutchinson's interpretation of the statistics is correct, do you believe that Carmichael's predictions should be dismissed or should strict policies to prevent overfishing still be implemented? Why or why not?

4. Of the threats to the world's oceans and sea life explored in this chapter, which do you think is the most serious? Explain, citing from the viewpoints.

Chapter 2

1. Michael Crye claims that voluntary standards set by the cruise ship industry are adequate to protect the marine environment. Sam Farr disagrees. How do the authors' affiliations shape their arguments? Do these affiliations influence which viewpoint you think is more persuasive? Why or why not?

2. Andrew Myers argues that fertilizing the oceans with iron is an unproven and potentially dangerous way to address global warming. Do you think that Dan Whaley, Margaret Leinen, and Kevin Whilden adequately answer Myers's concerns in their viewpoint? Citing evidence from the viewpoints, explain why or why not.

3. According to Benjamin and Daniel Friedman, to help protect the world's oceans, the United States should ratify the U.N. Convention on the Law of the Sea. Frank J. Gaffney Jr. argues against ratification. He fears that the treaty will threaten U.S. sovereignty and security. Do you think that the Friedmans adequately address Gaffney's concerns? Explain why or why not, citing from the viewpoints.

4. What commonalities can you find in the rhetoric used by the authors on both sides of the debate over what ocean policies are best? Which rhetorical strategies do you find most persuasive? Citing from the viewpoints, explain your answer.

Chapter 3

1. According to William T. Hogarth, one of the benefits of aquaculture is that it will reduce the pressure on wild stocks of fish. Ken Hinman disputes this claim, arguing

that the amount of fish harvested to feed carnivorous farmed fish depletes more fish than it produces and is therefore unsustainable. Which argument do you find more persuasive? Citing evidence from the viewpoints, explain why.

2. In response to claims that fishing practices such as bottom trawling are destructive Nils Stolpe compares commercial fishing to agriculture. Stolpe argues that fishing technology, like agricultural technology, is going to have some impact on the environment. Since people do not expect agriculture to have no impact on the land, he reasons, activists should not expect fishing to have no impact on the marine environment. Is this, in your view, an adequate justification for the damage that Joshua Reichert claims bottom trawling does to fragile marine habitats? Why or why not?

3. While the National Coalition for Marine Conservation (NCMC) does not dispute the usefulness of marine reserves to help critically endangered species, it contends that marine reserves do nothing to reduce the fishing practices that led to overfishing and the destruction of marine habitats in the first place. To support their claim, NCMC compares marine reserves to designated wilderness areas. In what ways do you think this comparison is apt? In what ways do marine reserves and wilderness areas differ, if any? Explain.

4. According to Ronald Bailey, tight government regulations do not reduce overfishing. In fact, he argues, strict fishing regulations increase dangerous fishing practices and promote cheating. Individual Fishing Quotas (IFQs) and other property rights, Bailey asserts, overcome these problems. Food & Water Watch claims, on the other hand, that IFQs do not reduce overfishing and by privatizing fishing rights, IFQs put fishing management in the hands of large-scale fishing businesses to the detriment of small fishing com-

munities and marine ecosystems. If the nation's fisheries are indeed a public resource, do you think the fishing industry or the government will best protect the public's interests? Explain your answer by citing from the viewpoints.

5. Of the policies to promote sustainable fishing explored in this chapter, which do you think will be most effective? Explain, citing from the viewpoints.

Chapter 4

1. For Ben Macintyre there is no defense to the practice of whaling. Philip Armour disagrees. According to Armour, whales can be protected without a complete ban on whaling. What rhetorical strategy does each author use to support his claim? Which strategy do you think is more effective? Explain, citing from the viewpoints.

2. Dick Russell maintains that antisubmarine sonar poses a serious threat to marine mammals. Donald C. Winter counters that antisubmarine sonar is necessary to protect national security and that the navy has implemented safeguards to protect marine mammals. Does Winter cite any evidence that these safeguards are effective? Even if these safeguards were inadequate to protect all marine mammals, do you think national security should be a greater priority? Why or why not?

3. To justify the display of captive marine mammals such as whales and dolphins, the Alliance of Marine Mammal Parks and Aquariums argues that parks and aquariums improve the lives of marine mammals through conservation, research, and rehabilitation. The Humane Society of the United States questions this claim and suggests that the real goal of marine parks is entertainment, not education. Which argument do you find more cogent? Explain your position, citing from the viewpoints.

4. How do the affiliations of the authors in this chapter influence their arguments? Does this influence make their arguments more or less persuasive? Explain, citing from the various viewpoints.

5. What commonalities can you find in the rhetoric used by the authors on both sides of the debate over what impact human activities have on marine mammals? Which viewpoints do you think are most persuasive? Citing from the viewpoints, explain.

Organizations to Contact

The editors have compiled the following list of organizations concerned with the issues debated in this book. The descriptions are derived from materials provided by the organizations. All have publications or information available for interested readers. The list was compiled on the date of publication of the present volume; the information provided here may change. Be aware that many organizations take several weeks or longer to respond to inquiries, so allow as much time as possible.

American Cetacean Society (ACS)
PO Box 1391, San Pedro, CA   90733-1391
(310) 548-6279 • fax: (310) 548-6950
e-mail: info@acsonline.org
Web site: www.acsonline.org

A nonprofit volunteer membership organization, ACS works to protect whales, dolphins, porpoises, and their habitats through education, conservation, and research. The society aims to educate the public about these mammals, also known as cetaceans, and the problems they face in their increasingly threatened habitats. Its publications include fact sheets and reports as well as the society's research journal *Whalewatcher*, published twice a year. Recent publications and action alerts are available on the ACS Web site.

Atlantic Marine Aquaculture Center
University of New Hampshire, Durham, NH   03824
(603) 862-3685
e-mail: dolores.leonard@unh.edu
Web site: http://ooa.unh.edu

The Atlantic Marine Aquaculture Center is a federally funded research institution whose goal is to provide the research and development necessary to stimulate an environmentally sustainable offshore aquaculture industry in New England and nationwide. The center studies stock enhancement as a tool to revive wild-capture fisheries. The Web site's publications link includes project briefs, reports, and journal articles.

Blue Frontier Campaign

PO Box 19367, Washington, DC   20036
(202) 387-8030
e-mail: info@bluefront.org
Web site: www.bluefront.org

Founded in 2003 by David Helvarg, author of *Blue Frontier— Saving America's Living Seas*, this environmental group uses local chapters to promote public awareness of coastal and ocean conservation. The campaign believes that grassroots efforts can influence national decision making. On its Web site, the campaign publishes excerpts from books, reports, and its periodic e-newsletter, *Blue Notes*, including the articles "A Dolphin's Plea for Understanding" and "Sustainable Life on the Blue Frontier."

Environmental Defense Fund

1875 Connecticut Ave. NW, Suite 600
Washington, DC   20009
(800) 684-3322
e-mail: members@environmentaldefense.org
Web site: www.edf.org

Formerly known simply as Environmental Defense, this national environmental group conducts scientific and economic analyses of environmental issues, including sustainable fishing and coastal development. Its "Oceans" link provides access to recent and archived articles and reports on current fishing, aquaculture, oceans, and global warming issues, including "MPAs: Safeguarding the Ocean's Cradle of Life" and "The Promise and Perils of Fish Farming."

Greenpeace USA

702 H St. NW, Washington, DC   20001
(800) 326-0959 • fax: (202) 462-4507

e-mail: info@wdc.greenpeace.org
Web site: www.greenpeaceusa.org

In addition to other environmental concerns, Greenpeace supports ocean and wildlife preservation. It uses controversial direct-action techniques and strives for media coverage of its actions in an effort to educate the public. On its Web site's "Oceans" link, Greenpeace publishes fact sheets on whaling, marine reserves, and other ocean issues as well as reports, including *Challenging the Aquaculture Industry on Sustainability* and *Freedom for the Seas: Now and for the Future.*

High North Alliance
PO Box 123, N-8390, Reine i Lofoten
    Norway
(47) 76 09 24 14 • fax: (47) 76 09 24 50
e-mail: hna@highnorth.no
Web site: www.highnorth.no

The alliance is an umbrella organization that represents fishers, whalers, and sealers from Canada, Greenland, Iceland, Norway, and various coastal communities. It is committed to the sustainable use of marine resources. It publishes the monthly newsletter *High North News.* On its Web site the alliance provides access to a library of fact sheets and reports.

Institute for Fisheries Resources (IFR)
PO Box 29196, San Francisco, CA   94129-0196
(415) 561-3474 • fax: (415) 561-5464
Web site: www.ifrfish.org

IFR conducts fishery research and promotes the conservation needs of fishers by serving as a bridge between traditional conservationist organizations and the commercial fishing industry. Its mission is to protect and restore fish populations and the human economies that depend on them. The institute establishes alliances among fishers, government agencies, and concerned citizens. On its Web site IFR publishes fact sheets on its programs and articles on current issues affecting fishers through its News/Events link, including news from its weekly newsletter, *Sublegals.*

Marine Fish Conservation Network

600 Pennsylvania Ave. SE, Suite 210, Washington, DC   20003
(202) 543-5509
Web site: www.conservefish.org

This coalition of environmental, scientific, and fishing groups advocates sustainable fishing policies. The broad spectrum of interests educates policy makers, the fishing industry, and the public about the need for sound conservation and better management practices. The Web site's "Catch of the Day" link includes articles and editorials on current marine conservation issues.

National Aquaculture Association

PO Box 1647, Pine Bluff, AR   71613
(870) 850-7900 • fax: (870) 850-7902
e-mail: naa@frontiernet.net
Web site: www.thenaa.net

The National Aquaculture Association is a trade organization for the aquaculture industry, representing both ocean- and land-based fish-farming operations. Its goal is to promote national programs and policies that further the common interest of the aquaculture industry. The association also fosters cost-effective environmental stewardship and sustainability. It publishes the report *Environmental Stewardship* and electronic versions of its policies and resolutions on its Web site.

National Marine Fisheries Service

1315 East-West Hwy., Silver Spring, MD   20910
(301) 713-2239
Web site: www.nmfs.noaa.gov

NOAA's National Marine Fisheries Service is a federal agency that is responsible for the stewardship of the nation's living marine resources and their habitats. The service assesses and predicts the status of fish stocks, ensures compliance with fisheries regulations, and works to reduce wasteful fishing practices. Under the Marine Mammal Protection Act and the

Endangered Species Act, the service also recovers protected marine species without unnecessarily impeding economic and recreational opportunities. On its Web site, the service publishes fact sheets and reports, and it provides links to current fishing issues and policies.

Natural Resources Defense Council (NRDC)
40 W. Twentieth St., New York, NY   10011
(212) 727-2700 • fax: (212) 727-1773
e-mail: nrdcinfo@nrdc.org
Web site: www.nrdc.org

The nonprofit NRDC, staffed by lawyers and scientists, conducts research and undertakes litigation on a broad range of environmental issues, including marine and coastal conservation. The council supports a strong federal role in environmental policy making. NRDC publishes reports such as *Keeping Oceans Wild: How Marine Reserves Protect Our Living Seas* and *Medicines from the Deep: The Importance of Protecting the High Seas from Bottom Trawling* and the quarterly *OnEarth* magazine. On its Web site NRDC provides access to these and other reports and articles on oceans, fish, and marine wildlife, as well as excerpts from *OnEarth*.

Ocean Conservancy
1725 DeSales St. NW, Suite 600, Washington, DC   20036
(202) 429-5609 • fax: (202) 872-0619
e-mail: rrufe@oceanconservancy.org
Web site: www.oceanconservancy.org

Through science-based advocacy, research, and public education, the goal of the Ocean Conservancy is to inform, inspire, and empower people to speak and act for the oceans. The conservancy strives to conserve marine fish populations, restore clean coastal and ocean waters, conserve and recover vulnerable marine wildlife, protect ocean ecosystems, and establish ocean wilderness. The conservancy publishes the quarterly *Ocean Conservancy*, formerly *Blue Planet Quarterly*, posting recent and past issues on its Web site. Also available are fact sheets, articles, and reports of issues of concern, such as *Cruise Control: How Cruise Ships Affect the Marine Environment* and the article "The Ocean Rules Climate . . . Climate Rules the Ocean."

The Property and Environment Research Center (PERC)
2048 Analysis Dr., Suite A, Bozeman, MT   59718
(406) 587-9591
e-mail: perc@perc.org
Web site: www.perc.org

PERC advocates market-oriented approaches to resource use and environmental preservation. The center publishes the quarterly magazine, *PERC Reports*, which presents a range of ideas and information about environmental problems. In addition to current and past issues of *PERC Reports*, PERC's Web site provides an extensive library of editorials, articles, and reports, including "Beyond IFQs in Maritime Fisheries: A Guide for Federal Policy Makers" and "Saving Fisheries with Free Markets."

SeaWeb
8401 Colesville Rd., Suite 500, Silver Spring, MD   20910
(301) 495-9570 • fax: (301) 495-4846
e-mail: contactus@seaweb.org
Web site: www.seaweb.org

SeaWeb is a multimedia educational project established by the Pew Charitable Trusts. Its mission is to raise awareness of the ocean and issues related to its conservation. SeaWeb publishes the reports *At a Crossroads: Will Aquaculture Fulfill the Promise of the Blue Revolution?* and *The Marketplace for Sustainable Seafood: Growing Appetites and Shrinking Seas*, as well as the monthly newsletter *Ocean Update*. All of these resources are available on its Web site. SeaWeb also broadcasts on its Web site the online radio show *The Ocean Report*.

Surfrider Foundation
PO Box 6010, San Clemente, CA   92674-6010
(949) 492-8170 • fax: (949) 492-8142
Web site: www.surfrider.org

The Surfrider Foundation works to preserve coasts and beaches worldwide. Founded in 1984 by a handful of surfers in Malibu, California, the foundation has developed into a worldwide environmental organization dedicated to the protection and enjoyment of the world's oceans and beaches through conservation, activism, research, and education. It publishes the bimonthly, *Making Waves*, the latest issue of which is available on its Web site, as are news and press releases on current ocean issues.

Whale and Dolphin Conservation Society–
North America (WDCS)
7 Nelson St., Plymouth, MA   02360-4044
(888) 699-4253
e-mail: contact@whales.org
Web site: www.whales.org

WDCS is an international organization dedicated to the conservation and welfare of all whales, dolphins, and porpoises, also known as cetaceans. The society's objectives are to reduce and ultimately eliminate the continuing threats to cetaceans and their habitats and to raise awareness about these threats and possible solutions. WDCS publishes papers, reports, and other literature on a variety of topics relating to cetaceans, as well as *Whale Watch*. Its publications are available on its Web site.

Woods Hole Oceanographic Institution
266 Woods Hole Rd., Woods Hole, MA   02543
(508) 289-2252
e-mail: information@whoi.edu
Web site: www.whoi.edu

Woods Hole Oceanographic Institution is dedicated to advancing understanding of the ocean and its interaction with the Earth system. The institution's publications include the biannual *Oceanus*, which highlights the research and researchers at Woods Hole Oceanographic Institution in news, features, and interviews. Recent and past issues of *Oceanus* are available on its Web site, as is an extensive library of fact sheets, articles, and reports on a variety of ocean-related topics.

World Wildlife Fund (WWF)
1250 Twenty-Fourth St. NW, Washington, DC   20037-1193
(202) 293-4800 • fax: (202) 293-9211
e-mail: piresponse@wwfus.org
Web site: www.worldwildlife.org

WWF is a global organization acting locally through a network of offices. The largest privately supported international conservation organization, WWF is dedicated to protecting the world's wildlife and wildlands. WWF directs its conservation efforts toward protecting endangered spaces, saving endangered species, and addressing global threats. Its "Wave Forward" links Web users to fact sheets and articles on current issues related to marine life, oceans, and coastal regions.

Bibliography of Books

Shimshon Belkin and Rita R. Colwell, eds. *Oceans and Health: Pathogens in the Marine Environment*. London: Springer Science+Business Media, 2006.

Theresa M. Bert, ed. *Ecological and Genetic Implications of Aquaculture Activities*. Dordrecht, Netherlands: Springer, 2007.

Carl Cater and Eriet Cater *Marine Ecotourism: Between the Devil and the Deep Blue Sea*. Cambridge, MA: CABI, 2007.

Charles Clover *The End of the Line: How Overfishing Is Changing the World and What We Eat*. London: Ebury, 2004.

James A. Estes, ed. *Whales, Whaling, and Ocean Ecosystems*. Berkeley and Los Angeles: University of California Press, 2006.

Nick Gales, Mark Hindell, and Roger Kirkwood, eds. *Marine Mammals: Fisheries, Tourism, and Management Issues*. London: Eurospan, 2003.

Alexander Gillespie *Whaling Diplomacy: Defining Issues in International Environmental Law*. Northampton, MA: Edward Elgar, 2005.

Jen Green *Saving Oceans and Wetlands*. North Mankato, MN: Chrysalis Education, 2004.

Sharon Guynup, ed.
State of the Wild 2006: A Global Portrait of Wildlife, Wildlands, and Oceans. Washington, DC: Island, 2005.

Michael Heazle
Scientific Uncertainty and the Politics of Whaling. Seattle: University of Washington Press, 2006.

Gene S. Helfman
Fish Conservation: A Guide to Understanding and Restoring Aquatic Biodiversity and Fishery Resources. Washington, DC: Island, 2007.

Marianne Holmer, ed.
Aquaculture in the Ecosystem. Dordrecht, Netherlands: Springer, 2008.

John Charles Kunich
Killing Our Oceans: Dealing with the Mass Extinction of Marine Life. Westport, CT: Praeger, 2006.

Nobuyuki Miyazaki, Zafar Adeel, and Kouichi Ohwada
Mankind and the Oceans. New York: United Nations University Press, 2005.

Paul Molyneaux
Swimming in Circles: Aquaculture and the End of Wild Oceans. New York: Thunder's Mouth, 2007.

National Research Council
Ocean Noise and Marine Mammals. Washington, DC: National Academies Press, 2003.

Jonathan T. Phinney, ed.
Coral Reefs and Climate Change: Science and Management. Washington, DC: American Geophysical Union, 2006.

Donald R. Rothwell and David L. VanderZwaag, eds.

Towards Principled Oceans Governance: Australian and Canadian Approaches and Challenges. New York: Routledge, 2006.

Carl J. Sindermann

Coastal Pollution: Effects on Living Resources and Humans. Boca Raton, FL: CRC/Taylor & Francis, 2006.

Jack Sobel and Craig P. Dalgren

Marine Reserves: A Guide to Science, Design, and Use. Washington, DC: Island, 2004.

David J. Starkey, Poul Holm, and Michaela Barnard, eds.

Oceans Past: Management Insights from the History of Marine Animal Populations. Sterling, VA: Earthscan, 2008.

Index

microbial growth, 67–68
nitrogen production, 63
  from nutrients, 34
  slime creation, 61–63
  venomous weeds, 60–61
Russell, Dick, 186–190
Russia, 68, 118, 190

S

Schlafly, Phyllis, 122
Science Daily (on-line journal), 175
Sea ice loss, 175
Sea level rise, 19–20, 35, 72, 106
Sea-life impact
  acidification, 70–71, 75–76
  fertilizer runoff, 24, 61
  overfishing, 62
  See also Ocean threats
Seabed resources
  international responsibility, 25
  jurisdiction over, 117
  sediment composition, 78, 97
  vs. mining, 116–117, 121
  See also Overfishing
Seafood consumption, 14, 22, 127, 144
  See also Aquaculture
Sediment composition/traps, 78, 97
Sewage
  on beaches, 14
  blackwater, 90, 93
  cruise ship pollution, 84–94
  removal, 83
  run-offs, 24, 64
Silt impact on reefs, 37
Simpson, Grovea, 65–66
Slime increases, 61–63
Smith, R. J., 83
Snorkeling, reef rules, 43

Sonar. *See* Antisubmarine sonar
Soufrière Marine Management Area, 148
Species extinction, 30, 78, 178
Spotts, Peter N., 33–39
State of Coral Reef Ecosystems of the United States and Pacific Freely Associated States (report), 43
Status of Coral Reefs of the World (report), 46
Sterne, Jack, 28–32
Stevens, Ted, 32, 52
Stolpe, Nils, 56, 142–146
Suatoni, Lisa, 50–51
Sumaila, Rashid, 141
Surfrider Foundation, 31
Sustainable Fisheries Act, 151
Sustainable fishing strategies
  aquaculture, 129–137
  banning bottom trawling, 138–141
  IFQs, 160–172
  marine reserves, 147–159
  vs. fishing technologies, 142–146

T

Territorial use rights in fishing (TURFs), 165
Total allowable catch (TAC), 160, 169
Trivedi, Bijal P., 147–152
Turner, John, 123

U

Union of Concerned Scientists (UCS), 19–20
United Nations
  bottom trawling regulations, 139

233